P9-CBJ-040

The Pocket
Guide to

Selling
Greatness

Open More Doors. Close More Sales.

Property of:
Follett
Training and Development Department

The Pocket Guide to

Selling Greatness

Gerhard Gschwandtner
Founder and Publisher of *Selling Power*

McGRAW-HILL

New York   Chicago   San Francisco   Lisbon   London   Madrid   Mexico City
Milan   New Delhi   San Juan   Seoul   Singapore   Sydney   Toronto

The *McGraw·Hill* Companies

Copyright © 2006 by Gerhard Gschwandtner. All rights reserved. Printed in the United States of America. Except as permitted under the United States Copyright Act of 1976, no part of this publication may be reproduced or distributed in any form or by any means, or stored in a data base or retrieval system, without the prior written permission of the publisher.

1 2 3 4 5 6 7 8 9 0   DOC / DOC   0 9 8 7 6

ISBN 0-07-147385-8

McGraw-Hill books are available at special quantity discounts to use as premiums and sales promotions, or for use in corporate training programs. For more information, please write to the Director of Special Sales, Professional Publishing, McGraw-Hill, Two Penn Plaza, New York, NY 10121-2298. Or contact your local bookstore.

 This book is printed on recycled, acid-free paper containing a minimum of 50% recycled, de-inked fiber.

Library of Congress Cataloging-in-Publication Data

Gschwandtner, Gerhard.
   The pocket guide to selling greatness / Gerhard Gschwandtner.
      p.   cm.
   ISBN 0-07-147385-8 (alk. paper)
  1. Selling—Psychological aspects.   2. Success in business—
Psychological aspects.   I. Title.
   HF5438.8.P75G789   2006
   658.85—dc22   2006007024

I would like to thank the following people who helped
in the production of this book:
Jim Madru for copyediting,
Nina Girard for proofreading,
Tama Harris and Janice Race for production.

CONTENTS

CONTENTS

PERSONAL GROWTH

MANAGING THOUGHTS

Rule your mind or it will rule you.

—HORACE

$\int$ ales success is not so much determined by what we say to our customers as by what we say to ourselves. Del Polito, a researcher who studies thought processes, once wrote that we experience our thoughts in streams flowing at various speeds.

Dr. Albert Ellis, a noted psychiatrist, found that we are capable of developing two or more streams of thoughts, sometimes flowing in opposite directions.

Thoughts, most researchers agree, have a powerful effect on our emotions, decisions, and actions. Many consider thinking as a manageable process, yet few effective thought management principles have been discovered and very few of us seem to apply them consistently.

The three most useful thought management tools are Awareness, Appraisal, and Choice.

Awareness comes from questions like "What am I doing?" or "What kind of thoughts am I experiencing right now?"

Appraisal means examining your thoughts objectively, like "Is this thought fact or fiction?" "What evidence do I have for my conclusions?" "What basis do I have for my assumptions?"

An objective appraisal can lead to healthy thoughts after a sales call where the customer did not buy, such as "I'm not the

> Awareness comes from questions like "What kind of thoughts am I experiencing right now?"

one that the prospect is rejecting. The facts are that at this time he has no need, and he's only rejecting my proposal."

Choice means using your creativity to expand the number of alternatives available to you. Choice allows you to change or reverse the direction of the flow of your thoughts.

If you've read this far, by now you're probably realizing that thought management is hard work, but so are successful living and successful selling.

Dr. Norman Vincent Peale, who spent a lifetime thinking about managing thoughts, readily admitted that managing thoughts is hard work. "But, on second thought," he said, "it's harder not to."

TRASH OR TREASURE?

*The man who reads nothing at all is better
educated than the man who reads nothing
but newspapers.*

—THOMAS JEFFERSON

In reading everyday news, have you ever asked yourself: "What in the heck am I reading? This is a terrible story! What an awful situation!"

Did you know that one "regular" newspaper article can create a mood of helplessness, outrage, or anger?

We know very little about the effect of information on our attitudes. We do know, however, that reading can create an endless tide of emotions.

Although science has determined the effect of nutrition on our bodies, we can't pinpoint how much positive information we need to maintain a healthy mind. Nutritionists know, for example, the minimum daily requirement of vitamin C. We also have guidelines on the maximum intake of salt to maintain a healthy body. But not one single psychologist knows how much "bad news" constitutes a hazardous level of negative information. Do you know your own tolerance for news items covering violence in minute detail? Do we know how much positive energy is needed to recover from the emotionally depleting news-shocker?

We have the right to expose ourselves to whatever information we want—that's our Constitutional right—but how about taking the responsibility for choosing the proper exposure?

> We have the right to
> expose ourselves to
> whatever information
> we want.

How about placing a value on what we read?

In selling, our attitudes are closely linked to success. Thus we know that negative information—if we let it influence us—can be hazardous to our earning potential.

We can't say that reading more than 800 words of "bad news" exceeds the maximum dose. Nor can we establish a minimum daily requirement of, let's say, 1,000 words of positive information.

Each of us is operating the most brilliant computer ever built—our mind—and every moment of our lives we make irreversible decisions concerning its input. Will it be Trash or Treasure?

ARE YOU FIT FOR SUCCESS?

A sedentary life is the real sin against the
Holy Spirit.

—NIETZSCHE

We were all far more physically active as children than we are as adults. Staying or getting back in shape is a wholly grown-up notion. But so is our tendency to let ourselves get out of shape.

For Dr. Ken Cooper, methodical physical exercise is the guiding philosophy by which he lives.

Dr. Cooper didn't come to his view of fitness and well-being without experiencing problems or pain. At one time he was as out of shape as any of us. It took a frightening experience on water skis to show him just how important physical fitness is.

Dr. Cooper's concept of fitness—and the enormous body of clinical evidence to support it—is impressive. Physical fitness, he asserts, begins on the inside, with our cardiovascular system. It is neither cosmetic nor transitory. Fitness can't be stored. Fitness is the result of ongoing, concentrated aerobic activity along with proper dietary balance.

In large part, Dr. Ken Cooper is responsible for the fitness movement that has swept this country over the past decade. His tireless work with countless patients, along with his internationally known fitness center in Dallas, has put physical fitness on the map for good.

No one can deny the benefits of being physically fit as we embark on our journey to success. Only regular exercise can

> No one can deny the benefits of being physically fit as we embark on our journey to success.

help us truly understand how physical fitness and success are intertwined.

Dr. Cooper's experience with thousands of people of all ages, combined with his extensive scientific research, builds a strong case that an ongoing aerobic exercise program will ultimately put the odds for reaching success in your favor.

Sold by this evidence, I decided to follow his advice and began to walk regularly, four times a week. It has become a pleasant routine that I now look forward to, since I enjoy the tangible benefits of a clear mind, improved concentration, reduced stress, and normal blood pressure. I've also learned that I can't walk and worry at the same time.

I am convinced that Dr. Cooper's philosophy of physical fitness from the inside out can create the foundation for a more successful you.

DISAPPOINTMENT
WHAT'S IN IT FOR ME?

Man must be disappointed with the lesser
things of life before he can comprehend the
full value of the greater.

—EDWARD G. BULWER-LYTTON

What were your biggest disappointments in the past year? What expectations or dreams did not get fulfilled? Think of a few more. You are now ready to figure your D/G ratio.

D/G stands for Disappointment versus Growth (remember, disappointment comes first, growth second). Here is how it works: Begin by listing your 10 major disappointments from last year on a sheet of paper. Then count the number of unresolved disappointments (the ones that still have a bitter taste as you think about them). Next, count the number of disappointments that have increased your strengths. Let's say that you still have negative feelings about that one large order that you didn't get (but felt so sure about) and that you had to fire someone (with whom you spent so much time—but he still didn't improve).

Let's also assume that you've managed all other disappointments well, so your D/G ratio would be 2/8. The first figure indicates that you have 2 disappointment management opportunities left. The second figure indicates your growth ca-

> Every time you manage your disappointments well, you'll increase your growth potential.

pacity. Since you managed 8 out of 10 disappointments, your present growth capacity is 80 percent. If you would add another unresolved disappointment in the first quarter of next year, your growth capacity would then drop to 70 percent. What does this mean to your chances of reaching your goals for next year?

Simple. To the degree you deny (unresolved) disappointments, you will deprive yourself of potential growth. On the other hand, every time you manage your disappointments well, you'll increase your growth potential.

"Preoccupation with success may be less important than the role of disappointment in the evolution of a career," asserts Dr. Abraham Zaleznik. His research of gifted leaders supports the idea that the way we manage disappointment may ultimately become responsible for our achieving success. That's reason enough to use disappointments as stepping stones throughout your career.

Disappointment is nothing but an opportunity in disguise.

LEARNING FROM SUPERACHIEVERS

In each issue of *Selling Power*, we introduce a Superachiever (Super = above, beyond; to achieve = to bring to a successful end, to accomplish). I see my role as the interviewer to act as a broker of ideas between the Superachiever and the readers of the magazine. It is for this reason that I spend about one hour of preparation for every minute spent in the interview (some interviews last as much as three hours). By the time I meet the Superachiever, I can almost predict the answers to a number of questions. So if I get the "predicted" answer, I am prepared to go beyond the "boiler plate" reply (used in previous interviews, autobiographies, or numerous books) and go for the real story. To me these interviews are personally rewarding and an invaluable learning experience.

In every interview, I look for two essential elements. First, action steps to success; second, the overall success philosophy. After having interviewed such Superachievers as Larry King, Dr. Norman Vincent Peale, Mary Kay Ash, Dr. Denis Waitley, or Bill Marriott, I realize that the action steps to success are universal, they can be applied by anyone, but the individual success philosophy can only come from one single source: from within.

If you would ask me to condense my insights after 100 interviews into one sentence, I would answer: If you have failed to consciously define a philosophy of success, you have unconsciously defined a philosophy of failure. Think about this. Read

> It's the lack of self-knowledge that stands in the way of finding the meaning of success and finding success meaningful.

the sentence again. You'll find that it is true simply because, if your life is not guided by philosophy, it will be guided by fantasy. Well-defined success philosophies will lead to great success in reality, whereas fantasies of success will lead only to great illusions.

What is the key to defining your own philosophy of success? Simple. For success to become meaningful to you, you must look within. It's the lack of self-knowledge that stands in the way of finding the meaning of success and finding success meaningful.

Many "Success Experts" believe that you can become successful by imitating the success of Superachievers. To me, this amounts to putting the cart before the horse. Imitation is limitation. You are bound to be disappointed when you try to reach success based on someone else's definition. People who imitate carry only images of the end product of success in their minds. They stick a picture of yachts or Cadillacs on their mirrors and overlook the crucial difference between the fruits of success and the roots of success. They see the end, but not the beginning.

Concentrate on nurturing your own roots of success. Take the first step and define your own success philosophy to focus your energy. Next, follow the Superachievers' action steps on reaching success.

Remember: It takes no more energy to reach success than to reach failure.

THINKING AHEAD

*Efforts and courage are not enough
without purpose and direction.*

—JOHN F. KENNEDY

Take a moment to reflect on your own attitude toward goal setting.

Mary Kay Ash, the founder of Mary Kay Cosmetics, once observed that most people spend more time organizing their vacations than their own lives. If you agree with her statement, you could take this idea a little further and say, "Most people only know where they're going when they go on vacation."

I think that goal setting is the most important process in regulating your personal and professional success. If you don't plan for the future now, you're bound to repeat your past performance with a little less enthusiasm and fewer chances for getting what you really want.

To succeed in life, we really need to set two kinds of goals: short-term and long-term goals.

Short-term goals are your task management tool, while your long-term goals serve you as a "meaning management" tool. There is an interesting relationship between the two: The more meaningful your long-term goals, the more effectively you'll tackle the short-term goals.

Why? Well, simply because meaning determines the type of commitment you put behind your goals. If your commitment to your goal is only in your head, you'll lose it the moment you encounter resistance. But if your commitment is in your heart,

> Never consider your goal as the final destination, but as a road map for your journey to success.

no amount of resistance can hold you back from pursuing your goal.

Remember that your goals should serve you and stretch you. Take the first stretching exercise to get what you want out of life. Write your personal goals and sales goals today. Then edit and revise them at least once a week. Never consider your goal as the final destination, but as a road map for your journey to success, because ultimately success is not a destination, but a journey.

PREDICTING THE ECONOMY

The end of the year for most companies means that it's crystal ball time. Sales managers are adjusting projected expense figures and trimming overly optimistic sales forecasts for next year. Corporate bean counters are working overtime. As we hope that the next year will go according to plan, we sometimes feel uncertain about the process of predicting the future.

Are we co-producers of a charade or co-founders of a new era of success?

Sure, we need a marching plan, a global strategy, a flag on the map marking our projected gains. However, at the same time we all know that the future is not a logical extension of the past.

No "right" projection exists that can be concluded from past victories or defeats.

The future is nothing but a moving target.

Instead of hiring more consultants and conducting more studies (or reading our horoscopes), we need to learn to accept uncertainty. Annual sales forecasts tend to overflow with confidence and certainty. It is highly recommended to sound certain in any sales and marketing plan; however, we know that the plan is going to be only as sound as the assumptions it is based on. We also know that when real life doesn't match our predictions, uncertainty returns. The key to success won't depend so much on our looking back or looking ahead, but on looking inside.

The most powerful forces of success can be found within. We all need to learn how to use them better.

> The most powerful forces of success can be found within. We all need to learn how to use them better.

Let's begin by accepting uncertainty instead of trying to overcome it. By accepting it, we make it an ally; by fighting it, we knock ourselves out.

The success secret for reaching our goals next year is simply this: The better we adapt to the uncertainty inside of us, the better we'll adapt to the challenges ahead of us. With this problem solved, never mind the business outlook, but be on the lookout for business!

GENERATING ENTHUSIASM

Nothing great was ever achieved without enthusiasm.

—RALPH WALDO EMERSON

I recently received a phone call from a saleswoman who had called me once before. She asked me how I was, and I answered the way I always do, "Terrific!" She was surprised: "I talk to dozens of people every day," she told me, "and I never hear such an enthusiastic response." When I told her that I know a lot of people who give me a similar response when I call them, she asked me to name a few so she could catch a little of the rare commodity called "enthusiasm." I said to her: "Isn't it strange that everyone is looking for enthusiasm and yet everyone has it inside of them? They all want to get it from someone else and don't realize that they can easily give it to themselves."

I gave her the names of three Grand Masters of Enthusiasm: the late Dr. Norman Vincent Peale, Zig Ziglar, and Dr. Wayne Dyer. She knew of them but had never read any of their books. This little episode caused me to think about the many interviews I have conducted with positive people and how their enthusiasm literally changed my outlook on life. When we started our magazine *Selling Power*, I wasn't too confident whether our publication would make it through the first six months until I earned about the humble beginnings of some of the great people like Zig Ziglar. I remember reading every single article about him and rereading his books before I

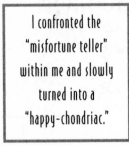

I confronted the "misfortune teller" within me and slowly turned into a "happy-chondriac."

called his office to request an interview with him. I remember telling myself, "He'll never take the time to talk to a little guy like me" and I was surprised to hear that he was more than happy to sit down with me to answer any questions I could think of. After I obtained Zig's agreement to be interviewed, I told myself, "I'll never be able to get any new information from him because I am not trained to interview people." I was wrong again. Zig's enthusiasm was infectious. He answered every one of my questions thoughtfully, and his positive attitude helped to eliminate my own "stinking thinking."

The interview was a full-blown success. It helped me realize that I needed to change my tendency to predict negative outcomes. I confronted the "misfortune teller" within me and slowly turned into a "happy-chondriac." People like Zig, Mary Lou Retton, Dr. Wayne Dyer, Lou Holtz, Spencer Johnson, Tom Hopkins, Mary Kay, Roger Staubach, General Norman Schwarzkopf, and many more have contributed their enthusiasm to *Selling Power* and the way I feel about life. "Terrific."

You may think that, as a publisher, I am in a privileged position to rub elbows with these Superachievers, but I sincerely believe that you can have every single one of them become your personal source of enthusiasm also. You don't have to sit across from them to capture their thoughts, to understand their ideas, to learn their principles, and to benefit from their insights. All you need to do is read their books, listen to their audiocassettes, or go through articles written by them or about them. You may realize, as I have, that by changing your heroes, you can change the direction of your life.

MENTAL GROWTH
THE GARDEN ANALOGY

Ideas are the root of creation.

—EARNEST DIMNET

Do you like home-grown vegetables? Like fresh string beans or carrots? Or a ripe home-grown tomato? Remember their taste and color? The smell of the garden . . .

Growing happy in life is a similar process. Happiness grows in our garden of ideas. Take a look at your garden today. What ideas have you planted? What seeds have you brought home from the store? Take a look at your stock of ideas. Are they fresh? Do you have a large assortment? Is each department completely stocked?

Never stop planting in your garden of knowledge. Keep your mind alert, curious, and growing. Unless you feel some sense of mental growth, you cannot be completely happy. When you realize that your knowledge and understanding have broadened, no matter how little, you have a sense of satisfaction that is impossible to describe.

But, as any good gardener will tell you, planting seeds and watering our crop is only part of successful gardening. There are the inevitable weeds that grow so quickly, without our lifting a finger. It's like in our garden of ideas, where negative thoughts seem to grow stronger when we ignore them.

Recent studies of failed corporations indicate that when

> There is nothing more exciting than an idea that has grown from a fleeting thought to a concrete, tangible reality.

companies neglect research and fail to discontinue obsolete products as quickly as possible, they begin their downhill slide to financial disaster.

Growing happy means work. We can't stop reading books, listening to positive recordings, or attending training seminars. As our knowledge grows and our storehouse of ideas expands, we need to keep pace with humility. We cannot be arrogant about our knowledge. We need to remind ourselves that no matter how far we may go, there is no end to learning. It is also good to remember that we are not learning for the sake of knowledge itself, but because we want to bring cheer to others with our harvest.

Cultivating minds is what growing happy is all about. It's amazing how our minds are keenly alert to all the freshness, wonder, and adventure of living. We all have the natural capacity to be enthusiastic and excited about the wondrous process that begins with a seed when we speak of the garden or ideas when we speak of the mind.

There is no higher feeling of satisfaction than the joy that comes with the sight of an overflowing harvest.

There is nothing more exciting than an idea that has grown from a fleeting thought to a concrete, tangible reality.

There is no better way to happiness than through the cultivated mind. Nurture it today, and soon it will be sprouting with ideas and your heart will be overflowing with happiness.

SELF-IMPROVEMENT

Every year brings new questions about what the future holds for us. These questions are born out of humankind's everpresent fear of the unknown.

Transcendental philosopher/writer Ralph Waldo Emerson once asked: "How shall I live? We are incompetent to solve the times. Our geometry cannot span the huge orbits of the prevailing ideas, behold their return and reconcile their opposition. We can only obey our own polarity." Emerson wisely suggests that we not be concerned with improving the world but rather with improving ourselves. As a side benefit, the world will be improved automatically.

Self-improvement has preoccupied the world's greatest minds since Aristotle. Great thinkers have improved the world's knowledge not by new ideas but by asking new questions. With each new question, new answers have been found, and with each new answer come new questions.

These questions, like the blades of a plow, turn over the fields of the unknown, advancing slowly, often burying old wisdom under a cover of newly found knowledge.

As we look at the daisy chain of questions asked by humankind's greatest champions of wisdom, we can find three key questions that can bring about ongoing self-improvement. Philosopher Immanuel Kant (1724–1804), at age 73, wrote in a letter: "Looking back I realize that my entire life's work focused on finding the answers to three essential questions. What should we believe? What can we know? What ought we do?"

It appears that self-improvement is more difficult than science not because scientists have to find new questions before they can find new answers but because self-improvement re-

> We need not be concerned with improving the world but rather with improving ourselves.

quires that we ask the same questions over and over again.

History, like self-improvement, is subject to forgetting and discovering. Case in point, 500 years before Immanuel Kant, Thomas Aquinas wrote about success: "We need to know three things, to know what to believe, to know what to strive for and to know what to do."

As we prepare to plow the field called life, we need to rediscover the fact that although we can't predict the future, we can build it slowly, moment by moment, through our beliefs, goals, and actions.

PIN YOUR HOPES ON ATTITUDE

*There is no object on earth which cannot
be looked at from a cosmic point of view.*

—DOSTOEVSKY

In *Selling Power* we wrote on the subject of attitude. Judging by the many letters and comments from our subscribers, it was a popular topic. To further examine why our readers were as fascinated with the subject of attitude as we were, I purchased 100 Attitude pins from one of our advertisers and began to hand out these pins to visiting salespeople, customers, suppliers, and even to complete strangers. It was a most rewarding experience.

In New Orleans I handed a pin to a reception clerk as I was checking into the hotel. In return, I received a Junior Suite at no extra cost. A salesman who visited my office wore the pin to his next sales call. He told me that the pin brightened his mood and even led to an extra sale that day. Every one of his prospects noticed the pin, and that little pin became a welcome icebreaker on several cold calls.

One sales manager called me a few days after receiving his pin to tell me that it had saved his life. By a twist of fate, a few days after he received the pin, his wife received a devastating medical report confirming that she had terminal cancer. As he was sitting at his desk, lost in thoughts of despair, he noticed the Attitude pin I had left in his office. He pinned it on his lapel and wore it during the entire day. Gradually he began to realize that the only thing we can control in life is our attitude.

> The only thing we can control in life is our attitude.

During our discussion, he told me that it was as if the little golden pin had broken through the cloud of helplessness and sent rays of hope that he sorely needed to cope with his sense of despair and desperation. To the rational business executive, attitude may be a small reed to hang his hopes on, but it's the one of the few reeds he's got.

SAILING AND SELLING

He is the best sailor who can steer within
fewest points of the wind, and exact a
motive power out of the greatest obstacles.

—HENRY DAVID THOREAU

I love sailing when the wind is brisk. During a weekend trip one summer, I noticed how much the wind influences the mood of everyone on the boat. During a healthy breeze, the boat slices the waves swiftly, leaving behind an impressive, boiling wake. Spirits soar, smiles appear, and crew and captain enjoy the exhilarating ride.

When the wind dies down, frowns replace the smiles, and the crew starts to find fault with the sun, the boat, or themselves. It seems that when the sails are full, the mind is filled with anticipation, and when the sails begin to luff, spirits dampen.

In the profession of selling, a similar phenomenon occurs. When the right wind is blowing, we're rushing forward. Anticipating success, we move on to bury our competitors in a sea of bubbling whitecaps.

It's thrilling to land a big order and to turn around in a rush of triumph and confidence, only to top off the day with another sale. But if we lose our momentum, and if the sails slacken, we're entering the doldrums and begin to question our mission as well as our competence.

A good sales manager's expectation acts like a swift breeze, keeping the crew humming, focused, ready for action, and totally absorbed in the process of reaching the destination. Unfortunately, some salespeople need more than a swift breeze, yet others move forward on their own. It's up to the manager to find the right setting on the wind machine to deliver everything from a gentle puff to an icy blast. Sometimes a thoughtful one-on-one talk with a salesperson will keep the sails and order books filled. At other times an exciting incentive program or a skills-building seminar is needed to provide the necessary upward draft.

> When the right wind is blowing, we rush forward to bury our competitors in a sea of bubbling whitecaps.

But what if you don't have an inspiring sales manager; what if you are out there facing adversity and rejection every single day? How do you create that invisible force to move forward?

Winners create their own atmosphere. We have the choice to turn on the heat or to stay cold; we're in charge of our energy, of our thoughts and goals. Winners create their own invisible field of forces and pressures. Their dreams, goals, hopes, expectations, commitments, and hard work fill the sails to move them forward to success.

AN EQUAL OPPORTUNITY PROFESSION

> Ginger Rogers did everything that Fred
> Astaire did. She just did it backwards and
> in high heels.
>
> —ATTRIBUTED TO FAITH
> WHITTLESEY, LINDA ELLERBEE,
> AND ANN RICHARDS

s the publisher of *Selling Power*, I have received more than a few letters asking for more stories about women sales achievers. With more and more women entering the sales field, these requests became an interesting challenge for *Selling Power*.

We contacted dozens of highly successful women: Liz Claiborne, Estee Lauder, Katharine Graham, and Jeanne Kirkpatrick, to name a few. Each time our request was answered with a polite rejection letter. Each time we received a rejection letter, we went back to the drawing board and did more research. When we looked into corporate directors, we realized that within the top 1,000 U.S. corporations, there is not a single woman holding the title of CEO. When we polled a cross section of our female readers, we found a great need for stories about successful women as role models for personal achievement, career success, sales, and management. When we talked to heads of asso-

> Successful women tend to be more inclined to encourage others to find their own greatness.

ciations of many different industries, we heard a familiar complaint: not enough women speakers, not enough women to select for awards, etc. Even more interesting was that when we researched the number of interviews given by successful women, we found that successful women tend to give far fewer interviews than men. Is it that successful women enjoy the process of achieving more than they enjoy talking about what they've achieved?

When we talked to speakers' bureaus that book speakers for conventions and sales meetings, one manager commented about the same issue, "Public speaking is a male-dominated field, and I sometimes wonder how many speakers really travel across the country with the mission to deliver their message and how many leave their homes to meet with an audience to get their egos massaged." This may be a generalization, but while successful men are more motivated to speak in public about what they've achieved, successful women tend to be more inclined to encourage others to find their own greatness on a one-on-one basis.

Selling is a level playing field. Selling recognizes neither economic background, cultural or racial heritage, education advantages, nor gender. Selling represents an abundance of opportunities that can lead to unprecedented achievements. Studies of successful women in selling reveal that the master keys to success can be duplicated by anybody. 1. Be professional in everything you do. 2. Challenge yourself constantly. 3. Keep your body and mind in top condition. 4. Always deliver more than you've been asked to do.

WHAT MAKES YOU HAPPY?

Happiness is not a destination. It is a method of life.

—BURTON HILLS

Creating happy customers is a great goal, but who creates happiness for you?

One of the key goals of most companies is to create more happy customers. The logic is compelling. Since happy customers will give us more of their business, they will refer us to more of their friends, and as a result, we will do better. Plato once wrote, "He who does well must of necessity be happy." That thought brings up two questions: Are you doing well? Are you happy? If the answer is Yes to both questions, skip this page. If you think you are doing well but feel a lack of happiness, then we have two problems on our hands: 1. How can you continue to make other people happy if you are unhappy? 2. What can you do to be happier?

Before we go any further, let's define what we mean by happiness. One of the difficulties in defining happiness lies in our shifting awareness. For example, when we are completely healthy, we are not aware of our bodies. The same is true with happiness. When we are completely happy, we don't lack anything, and we ignore our capacity to be unhappy. It is only when we are unhappy that we are aware of both—our unhappiness and our longing to be happy. Many people associate happiness with pleasure. Although pleasure can lighten unhappy moments, happiness is the result of long-term meaning. Whenever we engage in work that we really love to do, we

> Whenever we engage in work that we really love to do, we will always lose track of time and feel an abundance of energy.

will always lose track of time and feel an abundance of energy.

What can we do to become happier? Instead of finding happiness for themselves, some people spend more time making others believe that they are happy. They delude themselves by assuming that we always become what we think about. They forget that happiness is not an act of will but an action skill.

Many unhappy people think that getting away from their troubles holds the key to their happiness. The daily pressures of holding a job, the inconsiderate demands of family members, and the uncertainty of raising children in a society riddled with drugs, crime, unemployment, and unethical politicians often wear down the most cheerful person. While trouble often spoils happiness, the French writer Montaigne suggested the bold idea that inner happiness can exist no matter how severe the troubles on the outside. Montaigne wrote in 1570: "When the city of Nola was ruined by the Barbarians, Paulinus, who was bishop of that place, having there lost all he had, and himself a prisoner, prayed after this manner: 'Oh Lord, defend me from being sensible of this loss; for Thou knowest they have yet touched nothing of that which is mine.' "

I remember conducting interviews with American pilots who were shot down over North Vietnam. Although they spent many years in prison camps, were tortured, malnourished, and deprived of the most elementary conveniences of modern life, they all felt sorry—not for themselves—but for their captors. Why? Because they knew that none of the prison guards had ever experienced freedom. Through it all, these POWs maintained their capacity to be happy.

Montaigne suggested that we all should reserve a sacred space in our hearts or minds, "a backshop wholly our own and entirely free, wherein to settle our true liberty." It is in this sacred inner space where we store our greatest treasures and hide them from decay or violence. This secret space preserves the seeds to future happiness.

What else, besides a healthy dose of philosophy, will make us happy? One proven way is the art of self-leadership. We can all learn from successful people around us. Because these people act different, they feel different. While successful people recognize their ability to direct change, unsuccessful people fail to change direction. While successful people clearly visualize their destinies, unsuccessful people only see their limitations. While successful people exercise their right to choose, unsuccessful people choose excuses as their right.

Self-leadership suggests that if we take charge of our minds, our actions will be purposeful and doubts will vanish. Self-leadership doesn't require superhuman strength, it requires only discipline and commitment. There is nobody as strong as you holding you back from being happy and successful.

LEADERSHIP

In the movie *Glengarry Glen Ross*, a hotshot manager tells his salespeople in a surprise meeting: "The good news is that you're all fired. You have one week to regain your jobs, starting with tonight. Do I have your attention now? We are adding to this month's sales contest. The first prize is a Cadillac Eldorado; the second prize, a set of steak knives; and the third prize is the street."

Two of the salespeople react to the manager's threats and seek revenge by hatching a plan to sell their prospect list to the competition. The manager's pep talk backfires, the boost in sales doesn't materialize, and even the top salesperson fails.

Sure, it is a Hollywood version of a high-pressure sales organization and a distorted view of what selling is all about, but leadership by fear is still alive and well in corporate America.

While reports about poor leadership are brought to our attention every single day, it is hard to find examples of good leadership. In essence, good leadership begins with self-leadership.

What are the characteristics of a good leader?

1. **Awareness.** Good leaders do not simply repeat the information that comes from the press, the grapevine, or the company newsletter. A good leader is a person who accurately reads the signals from the top and the bottom of the organization, understands the information better, and gives it a common meaning for everyone.

2. **Vision.** A good leader has the ability to visualize the future and its possibilities. Vision empowers the leader with a special kind of authority that isn't written into the

corporate organization chart. Followers find meaning in the leader's vision and use it as a guide for their actions.

> In essence, good leadership begins with self-leadership.

3. **Action.** Followers judge good leaders by how they act and how fast they act. They ask questions such as: Does the leader avoid confrontation? Is the leader able to stand up to a competitor? Does the leader reward competence? Does the leader ignore betrayal? How long does it take the leader to face tough problems? Is the leader able to make decisions quickly? Does the leader allow others to win and get due credit for their victories?

4. **Responsibility.** Leaders offer their followers freedom in exchange for responsibility. Average leaders expect responsibility; good leaders teach their followers how to act responsibly; the best leaders become role models for responsibility and assume responsibility for their followers' shortcomings or failures.

5. **Self-Leadership.** Good leaders are in command of themselves, and they exercise their talents no matter where they are or what challenges they encounter. Self-leadership is a key requirement for leading others.

6. **Respect.** Good leaders respect their followers and treat them as their customers. Had the sales leader in the movie *Glengarry Glen Ross* addressed his salespeople with respect and dignity, he would have earned their cooperation. Since he threatened his people, his followers responded with anxiety, hate, sabotage, and indifference. The key lesson: A leader who treats others as fools is not a leader but just another fool.

ROLE MODELS FOR SUCCESS

*People seldom improve when they have no
other model but themselves to copy after.*
—OLIVER GOLDSMITH

I believe that if we surround ourselves with successful role models, we'll have a much greater chance of reaching success. Do you study the best practices of great people to learn from their experiences?

Take J.W. Marriott, the chairman of Marriott Hotels, as an example. He owes much of his success to his father, who etched the theme of ongoing improvement into his son's mind. Bill Marriott far exceeded his father's success because he continuously studied the best practices of other successful people.

What purpose do role models serve in our lives? They point us in the right direction and show us where to apply our talent and energy. In the same way that a ship's captain relies on such navigational tools as a compass, radar, or sextant to determine the position of the ship and steer a course to his destination, we can use heroes or role models to show us what could work and how to succeed in many endeavors. With the knowledge gained from our role models, we can chart a new course toward our own success.

Role models carry mental seeds that—if properly planted in our minds—can lead to a fresh crop of ideas, concepts, strategies, and decisions that can improve our lives.

For example, when I interviewed former POWs, I was impressed by their courage and endurance. When I interviewed motivators, I learned a great deal about their attitudes, their goals, and their high level of self-esteem. When I met with successful CEOs, I gained valuable insights into managing my own company.

Over the years I've found that for every one of our difficulties and problems, we can find someone who has applied persistence, determination, and skill to solve similar situations. Other people have realized their dreams—you can too.

> For every one of our difficulties and problems, we can find someone who has applied persistence, determination, and skill to solve similar situations.

To learn more from your role models, follow this three-step process:

First, decide on the areas in which you want to improve. Your improvement list may include personal success characteristics, professional skills, or strategies. Develop a master list of 10 improvements you'd like to make over the next six months.

Second, select two or three role models for each characteristic or skill that you want to improve. For example, to improve your ability to ask questions, you might consider studying Barbara Walters, Larry King, or trial lawyer F. Lee Bailey. To find suitable role models, go to your local library and ask for a reference book called *Current Biography*. It contains hundreds of concise biographies with quotes from interviews.

Third, write down the lessons you've learned from studying your role models. File your descriptions of your role models' "best practices" in a three-ring binder. Over time, you'll increase your own permanent success library. Review it often.

During the past 200 years, this country has created many successful role models. Try to benefit from them; choose new role models today, study their blueprints, and begin duplicating their action steps, and soon success will be yours.

CAN YOU SEE THE
OPPORTUNITIES AHEAD?

Age is a matter of feeling, not of years.
—GEORGE WILLIAM CURTIS

Although it appears that we live in a culture that worships youth, I really look forward to growing older. Before you turn a deaf ear to my opinions on the benefits of growing older, consider the alternative, and I think you'll agree that making the best of the inevitable makes sense.

The human race has never been as fit, as informed, or as mentally flexible as it now is. Medical advances have dramatically enhanced life. For example, a baby born in 1920 had a life expectancy of only 54 years; a baby born today can expect to live over 76 years. For those who live into their 100s, breakthroughs in fitness expertise and medical care have enhanced those later years almost beyond belief.

What makes life even more fantastic is our tremendous gain in the way we accumulate knowledge and distribute information. The world is exploding with new knowledge, ideas, and possibilities every single day. It's such a great time to live that I wouldn't accept a free ride in a time machine that went only backward.

Sure, it's great to be young, but it carries a high price tag. Let's take a look at the problems facing people between the ages of 21 and 26. First, a good college education costs $25,000 a year; second, entry-level jobs are hard to find, and pay is low for many years; third, automobile insurance is high (in fact, the risk of accidental death is highest for 16- to 24-year-olds); fourth, crime statistics show that homicides are at their peak between ages 24 and 34; fifth, employment statistics show that people between the ages of 21 and 44 need to take more sick days than older employees; sixth, data on mental health show that the risks of suffering from mental illness are much higher during adolescence and early adulthood.

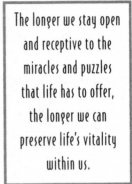

The longer we stay open and receptive to the miracles and puzzles that life has to offer, the longer we can preserve life's vitality within us.

I am convinced that growing older means we can get better, achieve more, and lead happier lives.

To learn more about getting better with age, we have interviewed Hugh Downs, ABC's Emmy award–winning former host of *20/20*. Hugh is over 70 years of age and as enthusiastic about life as a newborn. What struck me most about him was his relentless curiosity. After spending an hour with him, I realized that there isn't a subject that he would not be willing to discuss openly and intelligently. After the interview, an obvious idea struck me: Youth is really a question of receptivity. The longer we stay open and receptive to the miracles and puzzles that life has to offer, the longer we can preserve life's vitality within us.

As we are growing older and contemplating bifocals, we need to remember that age improves our inner vision. With age we gain a healthier perspective on life's challenges. We learn how to stay calmer and more productive under pressure, we understand ourselves better, and we take better care of ourselves. Yes, aging is a terrific opportunity for growing as a human being. The poet Longfellow put it best when he said: "Age is opportunity no less than youth itself, though in another dress. And as the evening twilight fades away, the sky is filled with stars, invisible by day."

ARE YOU IN THE MOOD FOR SUCCESS?

The University of Michigan conducted an important survey. The subject: How moods influence sales productivity. Since very few psychological studies address the issue of what salespeople can do to manage their moods effectively and productively, this research breaks new ground.

What do you do when you catch yourself in a bad mood? Take the afternoon off? Find a "symptom bearer" you can yell at? Or join the neighborhood bar for happy hour? It may be no surprise to you that such mood management techniques don't work. In fact, our research shows that these measures may depress you and your performance. Scientific evidence suggests that when you are in a bad mood, you can do three things that will lift your spirits and put you back in control—without costing you a penny. These mood management techniques are:

1. **Exercise.** When your mind is stressed out by bad moods, exercise the body. You'll literally burn off what got you steamed up.
2. **Work harder.** When things don't work out the way you expected, don't expect more from others; expect more from yourself. Make that extra call. Give yourself another chance to close a sale. Don't stew; go out and try something new.
3. **Talk to a mentor.** Talking to yourself doesn't help. Talking to someone else forces you to clarify your thoughts, which will readjust your emotions.

> Once people learn how to appraise events objectively, constructively, and optimistically, their spirits soar, and so does productivity.

Dr. Randy Larsen, professor of psychology at the University of Michigan, suggests applying some of the techniques developed by a new psychological treatment called *cognitive therapy*. This approach has become astonishingly successful for managing negative moods. Cognitive therapy was developed by Dr. Aaron Beck. Dr. Beck found scientific evidence that our thoughts (cognition) are mainly responsible for how we feel. What disturbs our mood is not a particular event but our appraisal of the event. If a customer who rejects your proposal puts you in a bad mood, you can get out of that bad mood quickly by reappraising the situation. Instead of saying, "This is not my day! He can't do that to me! What a jerk!" you can say, "He is only rejecting my proposal, and the more proposals I present, the more I will sell. Let's move on to the next prospect."

Once people learn how to appraise events objectively, constructively, and optimistically, their spirits soar, and so does productivity. The new science teaches us that it is up to us whether we interpret selling experiences in a hurtful or a helpful way.

Managing our moods is a vital key to success. Those who manage their moods stay on course; they are able to follow up on their goals. They stay in the optimum productivity zone—the mood for success.

WHAT NOW?

Before a recent takeoff on a United Airlines 767 jet to Munich, the captain went from cabin to cabin to deliver a short speech thanking people for their patience throughout tedious security procedures and for supporting the airline industry. During a break from his duties, I had a chance to speak with the captain. He shared that he lost his best friend, a fellow pilot who was in command of a 767 that crashed into the World Trade Center on September 11. The memory of this terrible tragedy cast a shadow of sadness over his face, and he added, "I guess we're never prepared to deal with such a massive disappointment. It has changed everything."

What changed? Airline traffic plummeted, stocks tumbled, mass layoffs followed, bonuses vanished, entrepreneurial dreams were shattered, and venture capitalists parked billions in safe places, pulling back from the market. These are the noticeable external changes.

The dynamics of disappointment have taken an internal toll that prompted millions of Americans to retreat, rethink, and refocus on what's really important in their lives. Disappointment is much more than failure of expectations. It is a powerful emotion that follows the death of precious dreams. Before September 11, we still believed that we were the masters of our destiny; we had high hopes that a better economy was around the corner; and we imagined that our country was a safe place. One single event shattered many of these illusions. We collectively realized that neither money nor technology nor military power could protect us from feelings of helplessness that will linger even longer than the putrid smell at Ground Zero.

> History teaches us that disappointment can throw us off course for our destination, but it cannot rob us of our destiny.

Disappointment manufactures rage. Rage at others for destroying our dreams. Rage at the fact that while we were trying to improve the economy, our situation grew worse. Rage at bin Laden, who masterminded the crime and inflicted overwhelming injury to our national psyche.

Dr. Abraham Zaleznik, the author of a 1967 *Harvard Business Review* article, "The Management of Disappointment," suggests that success depends to a great degree on how we handle the disappointments that are inevitable in life. To manage disappointment, says Zaleznik, it is a good idea to take time out to rediscover what's at our core and slowly rebuild hope. Dr. Martin Luther King, Jr., once said, "We must accept finite disappointment, but never lose infinite hope." September 11 has thrown the American psyche off course, but the American spirit has grown stronger, and the American economy is going to recover as we recover from the agony of disappointment.

Nobody has a magic formula that can fix the world's ills. All we can do is accept the new realities, have our shoes x-rayed before each flight, restore our faith in ourselves, and confidently pursue new dreams.

History teaches us that disappointment can throw us off course for our destination, but it cannot rob us of our destiny. As every sales manager knows, every disappointment gives us an opportunity to make another appointment.

THE IDEA OF IMPROVEMENT

Everyone thinks of changing the world,
but no one thinks of changing himself.
—LEO TOLSTOY

When Emperor Hirohito announced Japan's surrender during his historic radio address on August 15, 1945, Toyota had less than 10 years' worth of experience building cars and trucks. Just 24 hours before the war ended, an American B-29 appeared over Nagoya, where Toyota's plants were located. The first bomb missed the mark; so did the second; but the third bomb knocked out 50 percent of Toyota's vehicle-manufacturing operations. Within a short time, Toyota rebuilt the plant and opened new facilities, offering war veterans a fresh start. By 1949, Toyota's plants could produce 1,400 vehicles a month, but sales were slow. The company had difficulty collecting money from customers, and management had to plan layoffs. The labor union responded with a strike. As a result of the strike, most of the board of directors resigned, new management took over, and the company focused on launching new vehicles.

To help reconstruct Japan's industry, General Douglas MacArthur asked Dr. Edward Deming to teach top managers to adopt better principles of management. Toyota engineers and managers learned that giving orders and offering rewards or punishments was far less effective than was leading and supporting the workers in constantly improving quality. In 1955,

Ultimately, improvement mandates that we serve a community of ideas, not a congregation of egos.

Toyota launched the first entirely domestically produced passenger car, named the Crown.

Twelve years after the war ended, two Toyota Crown vehicles were shipped from Yokohama to Los Angeles. Miss Japan posed for pictures, and reporters were eager to report this curious event. While a few optimistic dealers labeled the odd-looking car a "baby Cadillac," predicting annual sales of 10,000 vehicles, the Crown could not measure up to the demands of the U.S. market. As technical problems multiplied, Toyota stopped Crown imports. To keep dealers happy, Toyota focused sales on the four-wheel-drive Land Cruiser until the extremely successful Corona was introduced. By 1971, Toyota had become the third-largest automobile manufacturer in the world. In 1986, Toyota started manufacturing cars in the United States. In 2001, Toyota produced more than 1.1 million vehicles in North America, with a team of 32,500 people and 500 North American suppliers.

What is the secret of Toyota's consistent ability to overcome adverse conditions? Members of Toyota's top management provide a responsible vision for the future, but their egos don't get in the way of their commitment to the idea of ongoing improvement. By adopting Dr. Deming's directive that managers must study the processes that make up their system and enlist the support of the people who do the work, Toyota has understood that managers must leave their egos at the door in order to tease out the ideas that lead to improvement.

Ultimately, improvement mandates that we serve a community of ideas, not a congregation of egos. Today, Toyota's market cap exceeds the combined market value of General Motors, Ford, and DaimlerChrysler, but top Toyota executives aren't bragging. They get more satisfaction from planning the next big improvement and from envisioning how far they will go than from measuring the length of their journey.

WHAT'S SUCCESS WITHOUT A HANDICAP?

We make our own fortunes and we call them fate.

—BENJAMIN DISRAELI

I am always amazed at how many people want to be successful without spending time thinking about what success is or what means they need to deploy to achieve it. The big question is, "What does success mean to you?"

Once I had lunch with Tom Hopkins, who defines success as "the progressive realization of a worthwhile goal." As we drove to the restaurant in his Rolls Royce, Tom reminded me that his father told him he'd never amount to anything. Tom never went to college, yet he has trained more than three million salespeople, and he feels fortunate that he can help others achieve higher levels of sales success.

Just a week earlier, I asked a cabdriver in San Francisco what success means to him. He was born in Rwanda. He said, "I feel so lucky, because I won the immigration lottery and could come to the United States. My father had three wives. I was one of 25 children, and I shared a room with four other siblings, sleeping on the floor. Having one meal a day was success. Now success means getting a good education. I have two jobs so that I can give back to my family and this wonderful country." When I arrived at the hotel, I checked out Rwanda on the Internet and found that the average life expectancy is only 45 years, and the average income is less than two dollars a day.

> Success is all about transforming so that we can evolve into what we were destined to become.

I also visited with Vinod Gupta, the CEO of InfoUSA, who came to the United States in 1967 from India. He grew up in a house that had no plumbing, no electricity, and no running water. His father, a doctor, earned only $50 a month. Today, Vin owns seven homes in such beautiful places as Hawaii, Aspen, Miami, and San Francisco. His collection of 12 cars includes two Porsches and a Ferrari. Vin's vision of success is to grow his $330 million company to over $1 billion. Vin has not forgotten his humble beginnings; he has helped build a college for women in India and has invested more than $10 million in charitable projects.

The cabdriver, Tom Hopkins, and Vin Gupta have something in common that may hold the key to their success. They all started with a handicap. The secret of their success can be found in the lifelong quest to move past their handicap. They all faced nearly insurmountable obstacles, which shaped their determination to succeed against all odds. They shared the dream of doing better than their fathers, and they share in their resolve to give back to society. It's interesting that the people who achieve success rarely have to read a book on the subject, yet they are the subjects that inspire books on success. Their stories prove that a handicap is like the grain of sand the oyster transforms into a shiny pearl. Success is all about transforming so that we can evolve into what we were destined to become.

CAN WE TALK?

Just a minute! Something's happening! Ladies and gentlemen, this is terrific. The end of the thing is beginning to flake off! The top is beginning to rotate like a screw! The thing must be metal! This is the most terrifying thing I have ever witnessed! Wait a minute. Someone is crawling out of the hollow top. Someone or . . . something. I can see peering out of that black two luminous discs. . . . are they eyes? It might be a face. It might be . . .

—ORSON WELLES

With these words, Orson Welles began his infamous one-hour CBS Radio broadcast "The War of the Worlds." The year was 1938; it was the night before Halloween. The broadcast caused a panic. People ran into the streets trying to escape falling into the hands of Martian invaders. This frantic reaction demonstrated the power of radio. But as millions of Americans purchased bulky radio sets and tuned into new programs, a subtle culture shift began. While people got into the habit of tuning into programs, they gradually tuned out people. Radio and TV became a means of escape that replaced storytelling, providing discussions and debates by proxy. The art of conversation began to fade. In the decade from 1920 to 1930, more than 300 new books focused on the art of conversation. Today, only fragments of that lost art survive. Today there are books on how to get attention, the art of small talk, how to listen, how to persuade, how to negotiate, how to argue, how to ask questions, how to read people's faces, how to tickle people's minds, and more minutiae.

> The world has become so fragmented that it appears we no longer recognize the art of conversation as a legitimate and wholesome endeavor.

The world has become so fragmented that it appears we no longer recognize the art of conversation as a legitimate and wholesome endeavor. Try to think of the last time you had a conversation in which you exchanged interesting information, examined views, and shared authentic feelings. When did you last have a conversation where thoughts began to flow spontaneously, you felt in sync with another person, and you walked away enlightened?

While radio and TV merely diverted people's attention from each other, studies show that new technologies actually inhibit our ability to talk and listen. A recent survey of more than 700 primary schools in England showed that the majority of teachers believe young children's talking and listening skills have declined in the past five years. The major culprits: the PC, the Internet, video games, and cell phones. One researcher said that many families no longer have lively chats but grunt at each other instead.

What the world needs now is a good conversation, says Dr. Theodore Zeldin. His book, *Conversation*, based on a series of BBC Radio talks, looks at the importance of conversation and how it can change your life. Zeldin believes that when two people are engaged in a good conversation, they don't just reshuffle the cards; they create new cards. To Zeldin, a sales conversation is about opening minds so that ideas and feelings can flow freely. In selling, open minds lead to new opportunities. Good sales conversations lead to satisfying relationships that offer meaning as a reward for the mind and money as a compensation for the effort.

THOUGHT LEADERSHIP

The real leader has no need to lead—he is
content to point the way.

—HENRY MILLER

D o you allow negative news to influence your thoughts? Is your mood regulated by the daily ups and down of the stock market? Do you get bent out of shape when you read news reports of how powerful corporate leaders manipulate financial information to enhance their gains? If you answered these questions with a Yes, it may be time for you to rise above the negative news and transform from an impressionable "follower" to an impressive "thought leader."

We do live in challenging times, yet this country has overcome far greater challenges in the past. Here is a story about a thought leader who trained a group of life insurance agents in Binghamton, NY. Sales trainer Hugh Wedge challenged his class to apply their new knowledge and skills in an all-night sales rally. They started operation "Paul Revere" at 7 p.m. and decided to meet for a midnight break at a diner to share their prospecting and selling experiences.

Many agents were surprised to find a large number of prospects who welcomed the opportunity to speak to a life insurance agent during their working hours. One agent sold a policy to a busy doctor at a local hospital; another visited every place he could find open, such as all-night diners, gas stations, and truck stops. He wrote four policies by midnight. Another

> It may be time for you to rise above the negative news and transform from an impressionable "follower" to an impressive "thought leader."

agent sold a policy to a truck driver at a depot. The driver introduced him to the two owners, who were interested in a substantial property insurance policy. He also spoke to several police officers. One of them bought a policy; another was interested in getting into the life insurance business.

One woman established herself in the cafeteria of the local hospital. She talked with the nurses, had three sales interviews, and sold three policies. One of her new customers gave her the names of 10 nurses, with a promise of a personal introduction to each one.

The waitress at the restaurant where they all gathered for their midnight break was a widow without insurance, and she happily bought a policy. After the midnight break, the group went back into the night, determined to return at 6 a.m. to tally the results. According to the report, the 29 agents worked a total of 209 hours that night, made 227 calls, concluded 125 successful sales interviews, and closed 61 sales. While other agents slept through the night, these 29 salespeople proved to themselves and their companies that there are no obstacles for those who are willing to put in the effort.

This story took place in 1949, when America's coal and steel industries went on strike and the economy retracted unexpectedly. The big news headline that year was about the Soviet Union testing its first atomic bomb. People were worried about the threat of nuclear war. Teachers began emergency drills, and children had to hide under their desks. If these insurance agents had been impressionable followers, they'd have stayed up all night digging bomb shelters. Undaunted by what happened in their troublesome world, these thought leaders followed their ambitions and met with uncommon success.

HOW TO STOP A TRAIN

*Nothing is impossible; there are ways
which lead to everything; and if we had
sufficient will we should always have
sufficient means.*

—FRANCOIS DE LA
ROCHEFOUCAULD

One evening I approached the Amtrak ticket counter at Penn Station in New York City at exactly 6 p.m. and asked, "When is the next Metroliner to D.C.?"

The agent said, "If you want to make a break for the 6 p.m., it's leaving in two minutes."

I said, "Let's give it a shot." I handed him my credit card, signed the slip, got the ticket within 20 seconds, and hurried to the gate dragging my luggage through the crowd. Another 30 seconds later, I skipped every other step on my way down the escalator. I thought that I had made it, since there was a train on each side of the tracks, but both had their doors closed. I asked an Amtrak official, "Which train goes to D.C.?"

"The one that's leaving behind you," he said.

I wheeled around, and sure enough, my Metroliner was rolling slowly down the tracks, as one car after another passed me by. For a split second I thought about taking the next train, but for some reason I didn't want to give up. As I watched the slowly moving train, I noticed an open car door and a conductor gripping the handrail. I made eye contact with him and asked, "How are you doing? Going to D.C.?"

He said, "Yes."

I followed the moving train, pulling my luggage along, and asked with a grin, "Would you mind if I join you?"

He said, "Let me see what I can do." He buzzed the engineer and asked, "Can you hold for one more customer?" Then he told me, "Continue walking, if he decides to stop, then you can come in."

As I hurried along the gate, I noticed people staring at me, wondering what would happen next. After I walked for about 20 more yards, the train came to a stop, and the conductor invited me to step on the train. With a big smile, I thanked him for making my day and entered the compartment. As I took my seat, I noticed that two more passengers had followed me, and they were thrilled to get on board. They asked, "How in the world did you get him to stop the train?"

> Selling requires an open mind that allows you to connect with people, no matter who they are, no matter how much money, knowledge, or power they possess.

I told them, "It was simple; all I had to do was ask." As I enjoyed the ride back to D.C., I thought about the many situations where I've used this principle. I have been able to visit with more than 100 nationally known VIPs to get great cover stories for our magazine. I've been honored to attend a private dinner with former President Bush and played golf with former President Clinton. I believe that selling requires an open mind that allows you to connect with people, no matter who they are, no matter how much money, knowledge, or power they possess. Selling demands a state of mind where we are open to all opportunities and unafraid to ask for what some people might think is totally impossible.

THE "BODY" POLITIC

A *good laugh is sunshine in a house.*

—WILLIAM MAKEPEACE

THACKERAY

We tend to judge people less by what they say and more by what they communicate nonverbally. Research by Dr. Albert Mehrabian at UCLA has shown that feelings and attitudes are communicated 7 percent with words, 38 percent with tone of voice, and 55 percent nonverbally. Salespeople don't always realize that they are walking billboards continuously flashing messages that can range from confidence to insecurity, from exuberance to arrogance, from trust to suspicion.

Here are some of the most important nonverbal communication channels that are worth monitoring during a sales call.

1. **Movement.** During a debate in New Hampshire, Ronald Reagan made a statement about free speech to justify the inclusion of four uninvited candidates. When the moderator asked, "Will someone turn off Governor Reagan's microphone?" Reagan, who had funded the debate, leaned over, grabbed his microphone, and said, "I paid for this microphone." While Reagan's statement was strong, his body language made it even more powerful. Grabbing the microphone turned the situation into a defining moment that ultimately led to his becoming president.

2. **Facial expressions.** While the facial muscles are easy to control, we are not always aware of how we come across. For example, President George W. Bush tends to purse his lips to relieve his tension. His smiles don't often go beyond a smirk, which some could read as a sign of arrogance. When President Clinton breaks out in a smile, he fully flashes his teeth, and crows feet appear next to his eyes. These signs of exuberance engender positive emotions in the audience.

> Salespeople don't always realize that they are walking billboards continuously flashing messages.

3. **Gestures.** President George W. Bush tends to swing his arms up and across his body, which makes him appear more powerful. Tony Blair brings his thumb and forefinger together to suggest precision. Like Bush, he uses stabbing hand movements to show that he's in control, emphasizing his points.

4. **Fluency of speech.** President Clinton can walk into any room, size up the crowd, and make the most profound statement about what the audience is thinking and feeling. President Bush sometimes lacks good grammar and syntax and often speaks in incomplete sentences. Although Bush is not quick on his feet, many people empathize with the contortions of his body language that prove he's not an actor when it comes to expressing his true feelings.

5. **Handshakes.** People who extend their hand with the palm facing down communicate dominance; people

who greet others palm facing up show submissive attitudes. The best handshake is vertical and brief, with medium pressure.

In sales as in politics, people don't always trust what they hear, but they nearly always make judgments based on what they are able to see with their own eyes.

PASSIONATE DREAMERS

I like the dreams of the future better than the history of the past.

—PATRICK HENRY

As the stories of highly successful business leaders suggest, dreams must be charged with passion to have a chance of becoming reality. Take Herb Kelleher, co-founder and former CEO of Southwest Airlines, who stands out as a visionary for creating the most profitable airline in the United States. Kelleher, with his hands-on, personal intensity, was a powerful role model for all his employees. While his competitors sat behind mahogany desks in their corporate offices, Kelleher regularly loaded luggage onto planes, filled cups with ice while flight attendants took drink orders, and entertained passengers with his down-to-earth sense of humor. What airline CEO would tolerate flight attendants who dress up as bunnies on Easter and wear turkey suits for Thanksgiving? Kelleher knew that any airline could copy Southwest's business plan, but no competitor could copy the fervent passion that's become an integral part of the company's culture. "Our people are so energetic," says Kelleher, "they couldn't be replicated."

Mo Siegel, founder of the highly successful Celestial Seasonings Tea Company, tapped into the same pool of passion as Kelleher. When Siegel was 21, he dreamed about becoming a millionaire by the age of 26 and reached his goal one tea bag at a time. He told me how he harvested herbs to create his first

> Dreams must be charged with passion to have a chance of becoming reality.

healthy blend called Mo's 36 Herb Tea and quickly expanded his line of teas, including the famous Red Zinger. Siegel made his first sales trips in an old Datsun, visiting stores and selling them on carrying his herbal teas. He infused his company with his dream of contributing to a better world, saying, "We believe that in order to make this world a better place in which to live, we must be totally dedicated to the endless quest for excellence."

Next, there is Michael Dell, who started assembling computers in his college dorm on the idea of building direct relationships with his customers. I remember interviewing Dell when he was only 27 years old, and his sales were just over $2 billion. What struck me was his boundless curiosity in looking at every business opportunity in a new way. Dell is a Zen master of relentless, no-holds-barred, ongoing improvement. One of his key management principles is a business-process improvement program where employees are encouraged to make the business more efficient and responsive to customers while giving individual team members control over having their ideas implemented in the company. In the internal document entitled, "The Soul of Dell," the focus is on winning. "We have a passion for winning in everything we do. We are committed to operational excellence, superior customer experience, leading in the global markets we serve, being known as a great company and great place to work and providing superior shareholder value over time." Unfazed by a long string of winning, the chairman of the $49 billion company has a relentless passion for reaching higher, claiming, "There is so much more to be done."

IS COMPLEXITY AN OBSTACLE TO YOUR PROGRESS?

*Far and away the best prize that life offers
is the chance to work hard at work worth
doing.*

THEODORE ROOSEVELT

Many of the largest sales forces in America employ armies of salespeople. Leading large sales forces in a fiercely competitive market is no small challenge. To ensure steady growth, companies must continually change their structure to meet emerging opportunities and improve their operation to satisfy customer and shareholder expectations. What sets the top companies apart is that they have a knack for keeping things simple. Progress demands that we reduce complexity. The big secret is that to move from complexity to simplicity is far less painful than the consequences of allowing complexity to dominate your process.

We tend to associate complexity with the things that are difficult to understand. For example, the buzz phrase *information overload* sounds complex, but it isn't. Every business generates an increasing amount of information that demands vigilant eyes to recognize threats as well as opportunities. There is nothing complex about analyzing information; it only takes quality time and organizational skills. When managers fail to

> We tend to associate complexity with the things that are difficult to understand.

recognize, analyze, and act swiftly on the available information, poor decisions will hobble progress.

The trouble is that we create our own difficulties, and the challenge lies in reclaiming simplicity. The path to simplicity often comes from establishing the connection between problem owners and solution providers. Many times, solutions to problems are closer than we imagine.

One day during a meeting in New York City, a bank executive at the next table shared with me that his organization has raised $500 million in funds for the United Nations to promote clean air. However, he admitted that it is difficult to get member countries to ask for grants to invest in clean-air projects. Sitting at my table was the ambassador of a Caribbean state. He said that his country had a project that would reduce carbon dioxide emissions by 80 percent, but they didn't have the funds to get started. I could not help but smile at the simple solution right at our table. By introducing these men to each other, their complex problem was on the simple path to resolution.

Another path to simplicity comes from understanding that people's theories guide their thoughts and actions. People don't always do what they say; people do what is in line with their theories. Complexity in organizations comes from allowing too many theories to get in the way of simple and decisive action. For example, when an executive operates on the theory that an organizational chart is more important than an effective action plan (as in the case of Hurricane Katrina), complexity will escalate. Albert Einstein once said that our theories determine what we measure. That may explain why complexity decreases in companies that use a commonly understood matrix. An effective matrix can be a great dragon slayer of many misguided theories.

To keep things simple, the effective leaders of the world artfully eliminate complexity; they are passionate about doing business in the least complicated way. They know that simplicity is a choice, not a chore.

WHAT'S YOUR DEFINITION OF SELLING?

Please take a moment to answer that question. If you could write your own personal dictionary, what would you write under *selling*? Here is what some top sales executives at *Selling Power's* recent Sales Leadership Conference offered:

- To persuade a person to take action
- A process of asking directive questions to help customers visualize how they could satisfy a need
- A process where a salesperson and a customer walk the road of agreement together
- The exchange of goods for a negotiated sum of money
- Finding a need and filling that need
- Selling is an art and a science. The science is the ability to diagnose a problem and find the best solution. The art is the ability to create the relationship and to co-create the solution with the customer.

Every sales leader in the room had a slightly different definition of selling.

Why is your definition of selling so important? Because everything a manager does will flow from that definition. For example, a manager who believes that selling is a process of persuasion will hire salespeople who can demonstrate great persuasive abilities. The hiring questions are likely to focus on the candidate's experience with persuading customers. The sales training program will emphasize closing the sale, and the incentive and compensation system is likely to put a premium on new sales rather than on retaining existing customers. A sales manager who believes that selling is all about building relationships will follow a different hiring process, design a different sales pro-

Why is your definition of selling so important?

cess, and come up with a different compensation model. In a sense, the sales manager's definition of selling will determine the sales culture of the team.

What's wrong with that picture? Plenty. The average tenure of a vice president of sales is less than two years. Each time a new sales leader arrives, a slight culture shift takes place. New players import new ideas that have worked well in their previous jobs, a new belief system takes over, a new definition of selling emerges, and soon a new sales process begins. The old way of selling quickly fades, and a new way of selling emerges. The trouble is that the new manager's way of selling is really another company's old way of selling—not proven in the new company and not easily accepted by its salespeople.

A company's sales culture should be a reflection of the company's mission and vision statement. Ideally, the "C" level of the organization should create a "sales culture statement" that defines what selling means in the organization. A sales culture statement should describe the customer experience, and it should outline the values that govern customer relationships. It could contain such guidelines as the prohibition of hiring salespeople from a competitor and outline the basic sales process. A sales culture statement creates continuity for the sales organization, encourages new sales managers to stay on the proven path of success, and gives salespeople the opportunity to execute better instead of having to change for change's sake.

PROFESSIONAL DEVELOPMENT

STINKING THINKING

> We have no more right to put our
> discordant states of mind into the lives of
> those around us and rob them of their
> sunshine and brightness than we have to
> enter their houses and steal their
> silverware.
>
> —JULIA MOSS SETON

Does a recession create "Stinking thinking"? The major problem of a recession is not the downturn of economic indicators; it's the downturn of people's minds.

A quick glance at recent studies will tell you that a downturn in the economy is always linked to a boom in drinking, health problems, business frauds, divorces, drug abuse, depression, and even suicides.

In selling, many experience a loss of self-esteem in direct proportion to their loss in sales or commissions. Although they know that they are often powerless to change the numbers, they do not always realize that they can change their unrealistic thinking and feel good about themselves. If you're down because your sales volume has gone down, ask yourself, "What does it really take to make me feel good?" A superficial response would be: "An unexpected order." But on reflection, you may concede: "Any positive action or thought."

The fact that business is down has not crippled you physically. Figures have no meaning; only thoughts have meaning.

> Don't let "bad" figures cripple your mind to the point where you forget that doing business is not everything.

Don't let "bad" figures cripple your mind to the point where you forget that doing business is not everything.

Remind yourself that what really counts in life is not what you do or how much you make, but who you are on the inside. A healthy self-esteem is the best recession antibiotic. It comes from the realization that only you can decide on your self-worth. A positive self-worth can boost your productivity by 100 percent.

Contrary to what many sales managers assume, true self-worth cannot be measured by adding up sales figures. Why not? Simply because you are the only one who figures and decides on your self-worth.

It's not the recession that's causing the stinking thinking; it's your figuring that is depressing; it's your thinking that's regressing.

You can stop your negative thoughts and feed your mind with positive ones. Positive actions will create a positive attitude. Quit moping; don't stew; go out and do. Decide on a boom in your mind. Get excited about your possibilities.

Try it and see how self-recovery will lead to sales recovery.

TELL THE TRUTH

Truth is the only safe ground to stand upon.

—ELIZABETH CADY STANTON

When I attended a national conference of sales training executives, I asked several participants whether the subject of honesty was part of their company's training agenda.

My questions drew a few blank stares until I talked to a training director of a company with sales approaching $1 billion.

He explained that he would start every sales training course by asking his participants to list the key criteria for sales success.

Each salesperson would name one or two items like "closing skill," "self-starter," "ability to handle rejections," "good listener," etc. But in 8 courses out of 10, explained the seasoned executive, the word *honesty* would not be part of their list.

"When they have listed 30 or more keys for sales success," he continued, "I usually ask 'How about honesty?' and I hear replies like, 'Are you kidding? A successful sales rep can't be totally honest.'"

The sales trainer, who had spent many years on the road selling, went on to explain how he would review in detail the advantages and disadvantages of honesty and estimate the damages to the company's image.

The late Senator Sam Ervin, Jr., of Watergate fame, spent a lifetime searching for the truth. He once told me: "The truth

> **As a general rule, people are the authors of their own misfortunes.**

doesn't come easily to everyone." He also mentioned, referring to former President Nixon, that "as a general rule, people are the authors of their own misfortunes."

In the preoccupation with success, we tend to overlook that our words—like the surgeon's knife—can be misused.

Perhaps we could explore the similarities between the practice of medicine and the profession of selling by looking at the differences between malpractice in medicine and malpractice in selling.

Judging by today's standard, malpractice in medicine doesn't always hurt the doctor; it hurts the patient and the insurance company. Malpractice in selling always hurts the company's reputation, and it hurts the salesperson twice: It hurts his pocketbook and his chances for professional success.

Based on this analogy, wouldn't it follow that telling the truth is the only malpractice insurance for both the company and the sales professional?

THE WINNER'S LAW OF 80/20

This essay should be co-signed by Dr. Denis Waitley, since the following thoughts are the by-product of a lengthy conversation about the subjects of pain, failure, and success. Together we discovered three new applications of Pareto's law of 80/20. (Pareto, an Italian economist, defined a number of 80/20 relationships such as: 20 percent of all employees usually produce 80 percent of the work.)

1. **On the pain of becoming successful.** Eighty percent of all people consider the pain related to personal growth as unacceptable. Only 20 percent are prepared to accept pain as a learning experience, alerting them to change.

   The 80 percent who want to avoid the pain of growing represent 80 percent of all failures. The 20 percent who suffer, but change and grow, represent the 20 percent who succeed in life.

2. **On the problem of avoiding failure.** When things go wrong in life, you can safely blame bad luck for 20 percent of all failures and subscribe 80 percent to yourself.

   The realization that fate authors 20 percent of all the misery we experience in life should not lead us to direct 80 percent of our efforts trying to control fate. If we spend 80 percent of our efforts on controlling fate, we're left with only 20 percent for controlling our lives.

   Winners invest their energies and efforts in areas they can influence and avoid investing in areas they can't control.

3. **On the problem of achieving success.** Eighty percent of the reasons why people achieve success can be

> If we spend 80 percent of our efforts on controlling fate, we're left with only 20 percent for controlling our lives.

found in personal qualities and skills. Twenty percent of the reasons can be attributed to external circumstances or luck.

The knowledge that luck is involved in achieving success leads 80 percent of all people to stop improving their personal qualities and skills. "What's the use," they say, "winners are just plain lucky." True, 20 percent of all winners are met by a smiling fortune, but it is equally true that 80 percent of all winners have cultivated and prepared themselves.

You can choose to gamble your life away, hoping for a smiling fortune to come to your rescue, or you can choose to increase your odds by preparing yourself. I vote for the latter because I believe in the old saying: Luck favors the prepared man and woman.

ARE YOU A PROFESSIONAL SALESPERSON?

We forget that the most successful statesmen have been professionals. Lincoln was a professional politician.

—FELIX FRANKFURTER

There are over 12 million salespeople in this country. However, in the eyes of some of the leading sales experts, like Larry Wilson and Tom Hopkins, only very few can be considered professionals—perhaps only 1 in 10.

Although amateurs and professionals may look alike in appearance and grooming, they are significantly different in the way they deal with a customer.

Where amateurs talk at the prospect, the professional listens to the person behind the prospect. Where amateurs are preoccupied with price and discounts, the professional focuses on customer needs and benefits. While amateurs leave loose ends untied, the professional follows up. In essence, the professional salesperson uses knowledge and skills for the sole purpose of helping other people, thus creating a true win/win situation. While amateurs haggle over who will get a bigger slice of the pie, the professional helps to create more pies for everyone!

As a result, the 11 million amateur salespeople in this country pay the price of mediocrity, while the 1 million professional

> The professional salesperson uses knowledge and skills for the sole purpose of helping other people.

salespeople earn a good living and the respect of their customers.

By now you're probably asking yourself, "How can I transcend amateur status?" You can begin with a commitment to professionalism. Only you can make this decision. And once you've decided to commit your energies to developing professional skills and knowledge, you will begin to avoid the problems amateurs create through a lack of commitment.

Many amateurs keep themselves from becoming professionals because their real career interests lie elsewhere. This one really wants to be a teacher; another one has dreams of running an antique store; and another one has frustrated ambitions of becoming a writer. The sad truth is that none of them is a professional at selling—or at anything else.

People always confuse the term *occupation* with *profession*. It doesn't matter what the occupation; if you don't approach it with a professional attitude, you cannot expect to be successful.

You cannot reach success in any field without first reaching the stage of professionalism.

MOTIVATING AND REWARDING THE SALES TEAM

In every work a reward added makes the pleasure twice as great.

—EURIPIDES

How do you motivate your salespeople? An effective sales manager knows that money is not the prime motivator to a salesperson; meaning is. In order to create a highly motivated sales team, we need to continuously reward the three P's of the salesperson. The first P stands for the performance. A good sales manager recognizes the value of good results and pays for productivity. This basic level of motivation satisfies the salesperson's economic and power needs. Reward good performance!

The second P stands for the position. The effective sales manager recognizes the value of the salesperson's position by creating job autonomy and support systems that add greater importance and opportunity to all sales jobs. Don't give just lip service by saying, "Nothing happens unless somebody sells something," but ask yourself: "What can I do today to get everybody in our company to support the sales team?" In this area salespeople don't want words but action. This level of motivation satisfies the salesperson's achievement needs. Don't defend the salesperson's position; reward it instead!

> A good sales manager recognizes the value of good results and pays for productivity.

The third P stands for the person. Recognize the value of each individual. Satisfy his or her social needs, the need for pride in belonging to your company, and the need for recognition in front of peers. Also, satisfy the person's need to see his or her picture in your company newsletter, the need for receiving a personal letter from the company president, or the need for your words of praise and admiration for a job well done.

Motivation is not a one-way street. As you cover all three levels of motivation, you'll realize that your investment is paying off handsomely. You'll see a dynamic sales team; you'll realize consistent above-quota results and realize that indescribable deep-down good feeling that you've contributed to something very meaningful.

Motivation comes in many subtle ways and speaks many different languages. As long as you cover the three P's of motivation, as long as you reward the performance and the position and the person, you'll be motivated too.

WHAT CUSTOMERS EXPECT AFTER THE SALE

*The fragrance always remains in the hand
that gives the rose.*

—HEDA BEJAR

How many times have you said to a business acquaintance, "I owe you one"? It's pretty common knowledge that we live in an era of back scratchers. If you do someone a favor, you can reasonably expect that you're owed a favor in return.

Although this is true in real life, this rule does not apply in selling.

As a sales professional, you probably feel that when you go the extra mile to sell something to a customer, the relationship has not only become solid, but also the customer now owes you one. It may come as a surprise, but in selling, the opposite is true. No matter how hard you have worked or how many concessions you have made, when you sell a customer, he or she then feels that you owe them a favor. Yes, you! Let me quote an expert. Harvard Business School Professor Theodore Levitt, in the *Harvard Business Review*, writes that the seller is at a psychological disadvantage after the sale has been made. I quote, "The buyer expects the seller to remember the purchase as having been a favor bestowed. The seller now owes the buyer one."

For many salespeople, I'm sure this comes as a big surprise.

> Even though you had to bend over backward to get the order, you now owe your customer a favor.

Some have even told me that they do not accept this premise—that the sale is a relationship in which each party gives equally. This may be true on an economic level, but it has nothing to do with the deficit relationship created by the customer's purchase.

The perception on the part of the customer is that you, the seller, have not only gotten new business but also his or her money. There were many other salespeople after the same account, but he or she chose you as the recipient. Therefore, psychologically, you now owe your customer a favor. Economically, you are even. Psychologically, you are at a loss, even though you had to bend over backward to get the order.

What can you do to fill the customer's psychological needs, now that you recognize the problem?

First, pay special attention to keeping the customer happy. Send a thank-you note, be sure to call to find out how the product is performing, and answer any questions that may have come up since the purchase. Follow up on that account as if the sale had never been made.

A very savvy advertising salesman once told me: "I always approach my customers as if I were applying for a job—even after the sale is made. They're my bosses—and I make sure that I fill the time between two paychecks with special attention and superior service."

DALE CARNEGIE'S SALES WISDOM

The curious thing about fishing is you never want to go home. If you catch something, you can't stop. If you don't catch anything, you hate to leave in case something might bite.

—GLADYS TABER

Last year I read over 200 books on selling. Among others, I reread a classic that should be on every salesperson's desk: *How to Win Friends and Influence People*. What surprised me was that none of the new books could hold a candle to this 24-karat Sales Gem. It's a model success book that has inspired superstars in business and industry.

Although the book was first written in 1935 (it is now updated and revised), it dispels the common myth that "the old ways of selling" are outdated. Too many writers and public speakers tell you that "selling in the '90s" is very superior to the old backslapping ways of the previous decades. Ironically, they go on to teach you some "new" technique that is nothing more than a rewrite of an old-fashioned Dale Carnegie principle.

"I go fishing up in Maine every summer," wrote Dale Carnegie in 1935. "Personally, I am very fond of strawberries and cream,

> When I go fishing, I don't think about what I want. I think about what they want.

but I find that for some strange reason fish prefer worms. So when I go fishing, I don't think about what I want. I think about what they want. I don't bait the hook with strawberries and cream. Rather, I dangle a worm or a grasshopper in front of the fish and say: 'Wouldn't you like to have that?' Why not use the same common sense when fishing for customers?"

That superb selling story has been used by countless authors. (Of course, they conveniently rewrite the paragraph and take credit for the "new" wisdom.)

Although many have imitated Dale Carnegie, nobody has succeeded in matching his unforgettable style. Always practical, specifically aimed toward the goal of influencing others, he hurries along in a fast-paced style, making each point with a memorable story, rounding it out and driving it home with appeals for action. Like his selling rule: "Get the other person saying 'Yes, yes' immediately." Carnegie explains: "When a person says 'Yes,' the organism is a forward-looking, accepting, open attitude."

How can you get more "Yes" responses? By using the Socratic method. Says Dale: "Socrates kept on asking questions and finally, almost without realizing it, his opponent found himself embracing a conclusion that he would have bitterly denied a few minutes previously."

Good points? Of course! Although it has been proven many times that the old ways of selling have long gone, it is comforting to know that modern selling techniques are firmly rooted in the past.

KEEP OLD KNOWLEDGE WHILE LEARNING MORE

aul Galanti, who was held captive for almost seven years in North Vietnam, spent what seemed an eternity in solitary confinement. Cut off from the outside world, the flow of information was reduced to occasional taps on the wall from other prisoners. One tap was "A," two taps meant "B" and 26 taps, you guessed it, meant "Z." Information traveled at a snail's pace. Galanti only heard of America's historic moon landing two years after it happened. Surprisingly, Galanti's mind never functioned better. He could recall just about any minute detail of his life and would remember every single prisoner's name as well as his personal background.

Recently, when we met with Paul for lunch, he reflected on how hard it is to remember things in a society where we are flooded with information every single day. Very little is known about the effects of information on our knowledge. Modern science developed a theory called the *phenomenon of interference*. Simply stated, new information interferes with the old, thus leading to the erosion of existing knowledge (retroactive inhibition), and old memories interfere with the retention of new ones (proactive inhibition).

It's really very similar to coastal erosion, where moving water is the eroding agent. While coastal erosion is brought about by the action of sea waves, mental erosion is brought about by waves of information that reduce the shorelines of

> Mental erosion is brought about by waves of information that reduce the shorelines of knowledge.

knowledge. (A quick test to prove this point: What was the name of the POW mentioned above?)

Information is like a coin with two faces. One side is the great builder of knowledge; the other, the great demolition expert of our memory. How can we counteract the forces of erosion? Here are six quick ideas: 1. Reinforce the shorelines by relearning, by going back to basics every single day. 2. Reduce the waves of information by watching less TV, by reading less junk, by absorbing quality instead of quantity. 3. Review what's important. Recall what happened after each sales call. Repetition reinforces knowledge. 4. Rest for a few moments after learning new information. Allow time for new material to "sink in." 5. Write down what you feel is essential, unforgettable knowledge to you. Write down your best closes, your best answers to objections, etc. 6. Review the purpose of absorbing new information. Is the purpose to learn something new or to reinforce existing knowledge?

Remember that knowledge erosion happens every day. It is not alarming to us because we don't remember what we once knew. Do something about it today. Wouldn't you hate to see your competitor succeed with knowledge you forgot to protect from erosion?

ARE YOU MANIPULATING YOUR CUSTOMERS?

*When the eyes say one thing, and the
tongue another, a practiced man relies on
the language of the first.*

—RALPH WALDO EMERSON

These days there is a lot of talk about manipulation in selling. Most magazine articles, books, and even cassette courses today emphasize the "nonmanipulative," "synergistic," or "consultative" approach to the prospect's needs. These books and courses seem to agree that manipulative selling is a thing of the past. Is it?

The word *manipulation* has many meanings. The dictionary definitions range from "artful skill" to "changing accounts to suit one's purpose." Today we seem to give the word *manipulation* one meaning: "To make someone do what we want him to do against his will or better judgment." Of course, this is counterproductive in any selling situation. But does this mean that manipulation does not have a place in selling at all? Oliver Wendell Holmes once said, "A word is not a crystal, transparent and unchanging; it is the skin of a living thought that may vary greatly in color and content according to the circumstances in which it is used."

Words are the tools of the selling trade, and their meanings change according to the circumstances in which they are

> Manipulating yourself to suit the situation will bring you closer to your customer and to the sale.

used. Tone of voice, emphasis, emotional atmosphere are all in play when a salesperson uses any series of words. How we say something is often more important than what we say. In fact, Dr. Albert Mehrabian's research showed that feelings and attitudes are communicated 38 percent by tone of voice; 55 percent by gestures, postures, and movements; and only 7 percent with words.

Take the simple sentence, "What is it that you would like to think about?" Read it aloud three times, each time emphasizing different words—*what*—*is it*—*you*. Can you hear and feel the different meanings when you change the emphasis from one word to another? What impact would those changes have on your customer? Superstars in selling can deliver the same sentence 20 different ways depending on the customer and the situation. They manipulate language in a way that harmonizes with the customer. But they never manipulate the customer!

Manipulating customers only antagonizes them. But manipulating yourself to suit the situation will bring you closer to your customer and to the sale. Salespeople who try to manipulate customers break the rules of ethical conduct and violate the rules of professional selling. Salespeople who skillfully manipulate themselves only break sales records.

THE 1,905-CARAT SAPPHIRE

> *Colors seen by candlelight will not look the same by day.*
>
> —ELIZABETH BARRETT-BROWNING

A Texas gem dealer named Roy Whetstine bought a rock at a mineral show in Tucson, Arizona, for $10. The seller, who displayed his stones in Tupperware containers, had found the rock in a creek bed near Boise, Idaho. According to numerous reports in the national press, the unassuming rock turned out to be a 1,905-carat sapphire worth $2.5 million.

Roy Whetstine admitted that he paid less than the seller had asked for. "He wanted $15 for it, but he settled for $10," Whetstine told reporters. After the purchase, Whetstine went to a gem cutter, who carefully removed the top outside casing of the rock. Whetstine immediately realized that he had bought the largest sapphire ever found.

Roy could easily qualify as the shrewdest buyer of the year who had the good fortune to meet a salesman without product knowledge. The unsuspecting rock collector gave Roy what I would call a "stupidity discount" of $2,499,990.

This amazing sales story contains several lessons:

1. Lack of knowledge is an open invitation for exploitation.
2. No matter what you sell, your product is probably worth more than you think.
3. Sometimes we need to translate the ancient Roman saying, "Let the buyer beware," into "Beware of the

> A 1,905-carat sapphire will look like only a rock to anyone who is only looking for rocks.

buyer." There are just as many buyers with low integrity as there are devious sellers.

4. A 1,905-carat sapphire will look like only a rock to anyone who is only looking for rocks. If we set our sights low, we'll end up with low results.

5. We all have to settle for less when we ignore the value inside of us.

Think of the many times we feel as worthless as a common rock, when we refuse to believe in the great potential inside of us. How many wait for someone else to discover the "carats" they carry within?

This story is really about your future. It can be as worthless as an ordinary rock or it can be as valuable as a diamond mine, depending on how many carats you'll be able to find, cut, and polish. We do not know for sure how many "carats" we'll find inside and how much cash we'll get for them in the marketplace. But if you want to improve your odds, improve your abilities to the level that will put you in the league of the likes of Roy Whetstine's record-breaking sapphire.

USE ACT "AS IF" TECHNIQUES TO SELL MORE

onstantin Stanislavski, a world-famous director, wrote an equally well-known book called *An Actor Prepares*. This great book, in addition to being one of the best for the profession of acting, is also a fascinating book for salespeople. Surprisingly, the book describes many useful techniques for improving sales performance.

Stanislavski advised actors to add more life to the characters on stage by acting "as if" the imagined role were real. One of the key methods for adding more life to the character lies in the realization that a new role does not need to be the beginning of a new experience but the continuation of a past experience.

In other words, the actor can play the new role "as if" it were a replay of one of his real experiences in the past. Given the tremendous success of this method employed by actors like Robert Redford, Jack Lemmon, and Dustin Hoffman, it can even become a powerful navigation program for our thoughts, actions, and feelings in a selling situation. By choosing positive "as if" assumptions, we can influence the outcome of a sales call. Here are a few examples:

1. When you present your product, act "as if" it is the most precious item in the world. For example, Ed McMahon used to sell fountain pens on the boardwalk in Atlantic City long before he became the famous television per-

> When you meet your next customer, act "as if" you are enthusiastic, even when you are not.

sonality on *The Tonight Show with Johnny Carson*. In his ambition to set new sales records, he learned to hold a fountain pen as if it were a fine piece of jewelry. This added more life to his selling performance and more income to his pocketbook.

2. When you meet your next customer, act "as if" you are enthusiastic, even when you are not. Mary Kay Ash, the founder of the international cosmetics company, advises her sales consultants: "Action creates motivation. If you act enthusiastically, you will soon feel real enthusiasm."

3. Here is another "as if" exercise: When you give your next sales presentation, act "as if" you are the best salesperson in your industry. To add more life to this new role, think of your own past experiences when you have handled a situation very well. Then replay this feeling of success and the sense of confidence in your new role, and you will soon become the best salesperson you can be.

"ROCK POLISHING– COMPLETING THE REAL JOB"

*He who considers his work beneath him
will be above doing it well.*

—ALEXANDER CHASE

I read in a science magazine that in the average Australian diamond mining operation it takes about 21 tons of rocks to produce 1 ounce of raw diamonds. It made me think about how much in life depends on our shoveling and overcoming obstacles before we can achieve shining success.

But wait a minute, shoveling rocks and removing diamonds is just the beginning; it leads only to raw diamonds. The real work, the cutting and polishing, is yet to be done. It's a delicate and tedious task, and depending on how well it's performed, the diamond will receive the appropriate grading that determines its price.

Virtually every job has two aspects to it: first the spadework and then the real job. In selling, the real job begins when we are face-to-face with a customer. Our value will be determined by how well we cut the deal and close the sale.

We often have a hard time accepting that in order to do our real job, many rocks have to be moved out of the way. As a consequence, two self-defeating behavior patterns emerge. One is that we get so frustrated with rock removal that we just focus on the real job and nothing else. As a consequence, we risk being

> We get so preoccupied with removing rocks that we tend to forget our real job in the process.

buried under a rock slide of unfinished business. The other is that we get so preoccupied with removing rocks that we tend to forget our real job in the process.

The only escape from this dilemma is to (a) accept that the real job is always buried under a pile of rocks that needs to be removed first and (b) seek a better balance between our "spadework" and our real job. We can't allow ourselves to neglect one at the expense of the other. We should remember that removing obstacles on the way to selling—no matter what your territory—is a lot easier than digging through 21 tons of rocks for 1 ounce of raw diamonds.

APPLYING GOOD IDEAS

Elmer Leterman once wrote: "The average human being in any line of work could double his productive capacity overnight if he began right now to do all the things he knows he should do, and stop doing all the things he knows he should not do."

Mr. Leterman implies that we're all standing in our own way on the road to success.

As you read ideas on the subject of sales success, motivation, and professional achievement, you may realize that many of them are familiar, but you have never put them on your list of "things to do today."

Why?

What prevents us from acting on good ideas? What makes us forget to apply those ideas that bring us closer to success?

The answer lies in our methodology for acquiring, storing, and using information. In our information-inflation society, we're conditioned to handle ideas like a warehouse that operates on the "last in, first out" principle. In other words, what's new today is often gone and forgotten tomorrow.

The paradox of our time is that we all complain of being overloaded with information, yet we're all hungry for more knowledge. We all suffer from too much information and too little knowledge about what to do with it. In fact, 80 percent of what we read, hear, or see during the average working day is useless and even counterproductive for reaching our goals.

The first step to solving our dilemma is to apply the same principles we've learned for managing time to managing information.

> We're conditioned to handle ideas like a warehouse that operates on the "last in, first out" principle.

Effective time managers know that the key to prioritizing lies in identifying what is most important and most urgent. Effective information management demands that we find what is most useful and what can be applied without further delay. Any information that doesn't fall into this category should be filed or tossed out. But immediately useful information should be put into practice every day.

One successful sales professional recently learned a new closing technique. He found it so effective that he wrote it 12 times into his daily planner to remind himself every month to go back to basics. He simply stated his key to success as, "Progress does not lie in capturing more new ideas but in applying the ideas that work best more often." It's no secret what we know doesn't count. The only thing that counts is what we do. Will you act on it?

THE IMPORTANCE OF PERSONALITY

If you have anything really valuable to contribute to the world, it will come through the expression of your own personality, that single spark of divinity that sets you off and makes you different from every other living creature.

—BRUCE BARTON

According to *The Hollywood Reporter*, of the 70,000 members registered with the Screen Actors Guild, 80 percent earn less than $5,000 a year. Only 3 percent earn more than $50,000 a year. It appears that success in the profession of acting is tougher than in any other business. Only very few actors become lifetime success stories. But those who reach success in the field are rewarded far above the compensations available to the captains of business and industry. Last year the top-ranking entertainers in America earned well over $100 million.

Why is it that we pay entertainers more than top managers? What do entertainers sell that other professionals don't offer? The answer is simple: Personality. Entertainers sell their unique personalities, which offer predictable and pleasing ex-

> Entertainers sell their unique personalities, which offer predictable and pleasing experiences to the consumer.

periences to the consumer. Webster's defines *personality* as the personal traits that make the person appealing. In today's world of selling and marketing, the word *personality* is "in."

Millions of marketing dollars are devoted to "personality research." Companies want to learn more about the product personality, the personality of the latest advertising campaign, and of course, their sales and service staff.

Products without personality fail, promotions without personality fizzle, salespeople without personality lose business, and service people without personality are viewed as part of the "customer prevention" staff.

It appears that modern marketing has become the story of the letter P: Product, Price, Place, Promotion, People, and Personality. The bottom line for salespeople? Simple: Persistent People Pleasing Produces Predictable Prosperity.

SEEK OUT DIFFICULT BUYERS!

Many salespeople have a little list of customers whom they dislike. Some have treated them rudely or unfairly. One may have gotten them in trouble with their company. Others have a habit of canceling orders, and so on.

A friend who has been in selling on the East Coast in a three-state region for over five years was given an additional state to increase the sales potential in his territory. After an extensive 20-day tour of the territory, he showed me his notes on how he was received when he made his calls. He was calling on business owners, general managers, and their secretaries. He made a total of 176 contacts in person and via telephone. Fifty-one prospects and customers could not be reached or could not be seen during the time period. He made 125 personal calls, which he classified as follows:

- Very pleasant and agreeable—9
- Friendly and courteous—31
- Businesslike but somewhat cold—56
- Abrupt—18
- Hostile or rude—8
- Missed appointments—3

He found that 20.8 percent of the prospects and customers he called on were difficult (abrupt, hostile, or rude), and 44.8 percent were somewhat cold. Although the salesman reached the sales quota set for the territory during that month, he felt that nearly two-thirds of the people he called on were difficult people. He soon developed an informal blacklist of prospects and customers who were just too difficult to see. Needless to say, we had a long discussion about his attitude for dealing

> **Dealing with difficult customers can benefit sales and character.**

with problem customers. I reminded him that if he made a specialty of selling to difficult customers, it would benefit him in both his sales and his character.

I told him a little bit about my job of interviewing very successful and very busy people for *Selling Power*. I soon learned that the majority of these superachievers have been labeled "impossible" by journalists at other magazines. As a result, I made it my business to concentrate my attention on this list of impossibles. Instead of developing a blacklist, I developed a goal list, and one by one, I crossed off names from the list of impossibles, and many of them have become good friends. One of them, Zig Ziglar, once told me, "The tougher you are on yourself, the easier life will be on you." Another friend, Dr. Norman Vincent Peale, mentioned that, "Every problem contains the seed to its own solution," and Senator Sam Ervin, Jr., explained (during an "impossible" interview) that "Problems are the diamond dust with which nature polishes its jewels."

To me there are no problem prospects, only mislabeled friends.

STAY BALANCED
AND MOVE FORWARD

Think like a man of action and act like a man of thought.

—HENRI BERGSON

hat are the two most important factors for setting and achieving our goals? The first is setting realistic, attainable, and measurable goals. If we aim too high, we'll get frustrated; if we aim too low, we'll achieve less than our potential. The second factor lies in achieving balance in our daily lives. Balance is one of the most overlooked success factors, and only very few authors ever mention it. Take any sport and think of just how important balance is to achieving mastery. In archery, setting goals is equal to the task of lining up the arrow with the bullseye. Achieving the goal, however, depends on the archer's ability to maintain balance. Just one wrong movement and the arrow will miss the target. It is the same in golf, basketball, or football: Dexterity and power depend on our ability to maintain balance. Balance leads to stability and consistency. The secret of all consistent achievers lies in their vigilance about achieving and maintaining balance.

Joseph E. Canion, former CEO of Compaq Computer Corporation, a company that went from 110 people to 6,000 in

> **We need to stay balanced and focused while we keep forging ahead.**

just seven years, was once asked how he managed to keep his company balanced and growing at the same time. Canion explained that the process was very much like a high-wire balancing act: "The job of a high-wire walker is to advance and to stay balanced at the same time. If you take your eyes off the wire, you tend to fall." In other words, we need to stay balanced and focused while we keep forging ahead.

The natural enemy of balance is speed. As we go faster, our fear of losing balance and control increases. I've seen skiers become immoblized on a downhill stretch and divers crawl down the ladder from the top of a 10-meter board. It is good to remember to seek our challenges that are in line with our skills and to learn from the masters who have gone before us. Risking too much is just as foolish as taking no risk at all. However, perfect balance (and freedom from fear) is only achieved by repeating the past, which makes progress impossible.

Moishe Feldenkrais, an Israeli physician and expert on body movements, viewed the human skeleton as a system of triangles. Feldenkrais sees a pair of walking legs as a triangle that creates a pattern of imbalance–balance–imbalance–balance. With each step we create an imbalance that creates forward momentum until it is stopped by the next step, which leads to temporary balance. In other words, to move forward, achieving balance is just as important as creating imbalance.

Achieving our goals means staying focused, creating imbalance, keeping balanced, and moving forward all at the same time. Sounds complex? It is. Many people fall? Yes! Many people drop out? You bet! Some even succeed and then get into trouble!

Achieving is not for the fainthearted. But given the fact that standing still means retreat and defeat, the small risk of steadily advancing is infinitely preferable.

CAN YOU DUPLICATE YOUR SUCCESSES?

> *The toughest thing about success is that you've got to keep on being a success.*
>
> —IRVING BERLIN

During a convention seminar for automotive dealers, one of the speakers gave this piece of advice to sales managers: "All you have to do to get out of a selling slump is to teach your salespeople to repeat their own best performance more often."

The speaker brought a puzzling problem into focus: "What causes salespeople to forget their own successes and lose the skills that caused them to be great?"

Dr. Norman Vincent Peale once said that a problem contains the seed to its own solution. We can turn this meaningful insight 180 degrees and say that every success contains the seed to its own undoing. People often believe that success only breeds success, but more often than not, success breeds complacency and arrogance, and it can lower our competitive drive. When success comes too fast, it often disappears as quickly as it came. I remember a salesman who made $1 million in commissions only five years ago. Last year he barely made $30,000. He lost his home, his family, and his self-esteem. Five years ago, hundreds of people listened eagerly to his success stories; today, only his creditors follow his footsteps.

Many salespeople have mastered the challenges of continuous success, year after year.

Charles Givens, author of the best-seller *Wealth Without Risk*, once told me that only after he lost everything he had (he went from millions to nothing twice) did he realize that it was easier to make money than to hang on to it. It seems obvious that becoming successful is far less challenging than staying successful.

There are many salespeople who have mastered the challenges of continuous success, year after year. Take Zig Ziglar, who is probably the best-known sales trainer in America today. Zig keeps himself in great physical shape. He keeps writing new, bestselling books and produces more and more exciting video and audio programs for the profession of selling. For the past 35 years, Zig has been a model of ongoing growth and success.

Duplicating one's own success seems to be the result of (a) our awareness of the laws of success, (b) our commitment to ongoing growth, and (c) our willingness to keep learning and sharpening our skills.

Erik Erikson once called the key conflict of growing as a struggle between generativity and stagnation. Stagnation leads to an erosion of our skills. People who stagnate become so involved with themselves that they become unable or unwilling to take on new challenges. They have bought the illusion that they have "arrived," and they feel entitled to being celebrated and waited on. Generativity, on the other hand, is the drive for renewal, the hunger for growing, the need for achieving our next level of positive transformation.

While the forces of generativity become responsible for advancing and growing, the forces of stagnation arrest growth and spur erosion. We all know that there are limits to our capacity for growth, just as there are limits to how much we can slow erosion.

People who have learned to duplicate their success have learned not to look at limitations; they focus on opportunities instead. Only if we keep our antennae tuned to new opportunities will we recognize them and grow with them. There is only one choice, a wise man once said: "If you plan to keep on living, you better plan on growing."

IS THERE A RECESSION IN YOUR MIND?

In many industries, selling has gotten tougher. In order to keep their businesses afloat, sales managers are demanding more sales reports as well as more sales results from their staffs. Tougher times demand tougher attitudes toward available opportunities. Therefore, it pays to remember the two basic strategies for dealing with life's challenges: offensive and defensive. The purpose of the offensive strategy is to win. The purpose of the defensive strategy is to survive.

Salespeople on the defense path look defensive; they sigh frequently; and they tell lengthy stories about tough prospects, insurmountable objections, and impossible selling situations.

Salespeople on the offense look alert, confident, and ready. Their stories have a slight hint of arrogance when they describe how they cracked the impossible account, how they found a group of 50 fresh prospects, or how they made an extra $1,000 by upselling an existing customer.

In combat training, fighter pilots learn that the opponent who shows signs of a defensive strategy won't shoot at them because he is intensely preoccupied with getting away from the danger zone. Salespeople who try to ride out the recession with a defensive strategy are so preoccupied with protecting existing accounts that they tend to overlook the opportunities for new business. As a result, they spend too much time with their customers out of fear of losing them instead of attacking the challenges and opportunities that are being pursued by

> Salespeople on the offensive look alert, confident, and ready.

their competition. Their main concern is to hang on and not to rock the boat.

The legendary Baron Manfred von Richthofen once said that success flourishes only in perseverance—ceaseless, restless perseverance. Von Richthofen's first hit deeply ingrained in his mind the lifesaving quality of a swift offensive strategy. Salespeople who respond to an economic slowdown with an offensive strategy win battles every single day. They invest extra time courting new prospects; their enthusiasm brings smiles to the face of the gloomiest buyer; and their sharp techniques lead to new accounts and higher market share.

The defensive strategy is fear-motivated; the best you can do with it is survive. The offensive strategy is driven by the craving for victory, and there are no limits to your possibilities. No wonder fighter pilots pick the eagle for their symbol, and no wonder some sales managers hand out turkeys to their defensive teammates and cash bonuses to their aces.

THE INCREDIBLE POWER OF IDEAS

Nothing is more dangerous than an idea,
when it is the only idea we have.

—ALAIN

We live in the age of powerful new ideas. Nothing gives more of a mental lift than the feelings created by one new and powerful idea. Dr. Jonas Salk once said that the moment an idea is expressed, it becomes a form of life with its own genetic code. Once born, it is up to us to nurture a new idea or to let it die. Some ideas are very short-lived; others grow steadily, gain worldwide acceptance, and live on for decades, even centuries.

Humankind advances through the power of ideas. One simple idea, born out of a single mind, has the capacity to change the lives of millions of people around the world. Just think of Edison's light bulb—over five billion people now enjoy the benefits of his unique idea.

Creative salespeople know how to harness the power of ideas. To many people, the process of creating ideas that sell appears mysterious, yet their minds are continually at work thinking, visualizing, daydreaming, and fantasizing. To harness the power of ideas, we need to ask ourselves, "What do I want to get out of ideas?" Without that question, we will go on producing ideas at random, dispersing our creative energies without

> In order to profit from ideas, we need to learn from three disciplines: fishing, nursing, and gardening.

hope for profit. In order to profit from ideas, we need to learn from three disciplines: fishing, nursing, and gardening. Let's discuss them one at a time.

1. **Fishing.** Many of the ideas we produce vanish quickly if we fail to capture their essence. Like fishermen who weave nets to catch fish, we need to create a series of nets that will help us catch the kinds of ideas that will lead us to new sales. Your fishing net could be a simple notebook where you write down idea categories like "new ideas for finding prospects" or "new ideas for handling objections" or "ideas for reaching my goals." Cast your net wherever you go, use your driving time to think of these categories, ask experts in your field, and soon your notebook will be filled with profitable ideas.

2. **Nursing.** If you fail to pay attention to new ideas, they will remain immature and will never be useful to you. If you nurse, nurture, expand, and develop your new idea, however, it will soon grow to a mature level. While immature ideas mean more work for you, mature ideas will make more money for you.

3. **Gardening.** Once your idea has reached the stage of maturity, it needs to be planted into the minds of other people. As with any type of gardening, you'll have to accept some dirty work like weeding, watering, and pruning before your idea will grow to its full bloom.

Some salespeople don't bother to catch, nurse, or grow their ideas. Often, their negative self-image prevents them from using their profitable ideas that will help them grow. Carl

H. Holmes once addressed the challenge of self-creation with these words: "Our business in life is not to get ahead of others, but to get ahead of ourselves—to break our own records, to improve our own methods and to do our work better than we have ever done before." The only way we can achieve that goal is by harnessing the incredible power of new ideas.

IT'S TIME TO ADJUST YOUR SELLING STRATEGY!

hen the economic pendulum swings toward a slow-down, we face a series of tough choices. Since the majority of economic forecasters predict tougher times, we've asked a select number of sales managers for their advice on how to cushion the inevitable rough ride ahead. Below is a sampling of their ideas:

1. **Don't put all your eggs into one basket.** Expand your customer base. This is the best time for getting new business because customers are looking for better ideas that can lower costs and increase productivity. If 80 percent of your business comes from 20 percent of your customers, you may be headed for trouble.

2. **Never be afraid to talk about money early on in the sale.** Don't waste your time with customers who don't have the financial muscle to back up their buying decisions. Remember, the decision to buy is only the first step of the close. It is better to close two smaller sales than to have one big sale slip away because the customer's financing fell through.

3. **No matter how tough competition gets, never compromise your integrity.** Even when your competition is fighting for sales with dirty tricks, don't lower your ethical standards. If you are in doubt about which course of action to take, get legal advice.

4. **Cut the fat out of your budget, but leave the muscle you need to keep your sales up to speed.** For every hour spent in meetings designed to cut the budget, invest an equal amount of time in thinking of new ways to increase sales. If you only look for ideas for cutting costs, your sales team will never find ideas that could double your sales.

5. **Upgrade your negotiation skills for dealing with collections.** Collect receivables with a carrot and a stick. Sell your customers on the benefits of paying, the troubles saved by sending the check, the advantages of a good credit rating, and the consequences of legal actions. Be friendly, listen to their stories, and no matter what they tell you, always come back with your demands for payment.

6. **Don't go soft when customers try to cancel a firm order.** Tough times will test your sense of fairness. Develop a positive attitude toward the job of "reselling the sold customer." Because of a new budget directive, the customer's boss often will veto a purchase order after it has been signed. Save the sale by reselling your customer's boss on the benefits of your product and on the necessity to stick with the original agreement.

7. **Make concessions when selling in a recession.** Rethink your offer. Can you add extra services? Extra parts? Extended warranties? Deferred payments? Better interest rates? Special options? A longer try-out period? A free loaner in case of breakdown? A free training course for the operation? A factory visit? Can you bundle products together? A three-year, guaranteed buy-back plan? Brainstorm more creative selling ideas today!

8. **Monitor your existing customers' financial health.** Always ask questions about their business plans, their

> Although we can't control the economy or our customers, we can control our attitude.

sales, their operating budgets, etc. Learn to look out for the sensitive financial indicators such as payment habits, key supplier payment terms, or bank credits. Remember that bankruptcies always hurt the ones who don't bother to check out red flags.

9. **Don't let the economy depress you.** Although we can't control the economy or our customers, we can control our attitude. Instead of listening to negative news or negative people, read positive motivation books or listen to motivational tapes. Regular exercise is the best antidote for feelings of depression. Taking a brisk, 20-minute walk three times a week is a great way to lift your spirits.

10. **Reject the values imposed by authority figures who try to tell you that "things will get worse before they get better."** People who hold an image of doom in their minds will always pursue a defensive strategy. People who see the "silver lining on the horizon" will always make the best of the situation and use an offensive strategy to get the business that's out there while everyone else is complaining about how tough things are these days.

IS UNCERTAINTY CHALLENGING YOUR CLAIM TO SUCCESS?

The man who fears suffering is already suffering from what he fears.

—MICHEL DE MONTAIGNE

The French writer Anatole France once said: "We live between two dense clouds, the forgetting what was and the uncertainty of what will be." From time to time, world events make the cloud of uncertainty grow darker. During times of uncertainty, customers tend to avoid making decisions, cancel purchasing plans, and revise payment schedules on existing purchases. Salespeople find themselves working harder, but many tend to get fewer sales and end up discouraged or doubtful about their future.

How do we deal with the negative force of uncertainty?

Uncertain times divide customers and salespeople into two groups. Eighty percent of all customers will delay making decisions and wait for the world to settle down before they will take the next major step. Twenty percent of all customers view times of uncertainty as an opportunity to move forward with new plans, ideas, and strategies. Eighty percent of all salespeople will allow uncertainty to erode their sense of purpose. They conform to the prevailing mood, and as a result, they begin to doubt their abilities, lose business, and miss valuable opportunities. These salespeople lose sight of

> Eighty percent of all salespeople will allow uncertainty to erode their sense of purpose.

what William Shakespeare wrote about the effects of doubt: "Our doubts are traitors and make us lose the good we oft might win by fearing to attempt." Twenty percent of all salespeople, however, view uncertainty as a great opportunity for pursuing and getting more business. Their optimistic attitudes constantly open new doors for them, and they find new business where most salespeople fear to look.

What can we attempt in a market ruled by uncertainty?

1. We can't change the world, but we can adapt to it. We need to begin by accepting uncertainty and avoid adding to it. Accepting uncertainty stops its ravenous growth.

2. We can't change feelings of uncertainty in our customers; we can, however, change our own feelings of uncertainty to feelings of confidence. Our own confidence is the best psychological weapon we can deploy to help our customers focus on our ideas and solutions to their problems.

3. In order to maximize our chances for success, we can use our selling time in a more focused way. Here are several quick ideas:

   a. Eliminate the subject of war, politics, and negative current events from your conversation topics. These subjects tend to arouse high interest, but they kill valuable selling time and negatively affect your prospect's attitude.

   b. If your customer brings up the subject, lead the conversation back to the business at hand.

   c. Reduce the amount of time spent with customers who habitually complain about these uncertain times and forever delay making decisions. While the average salesperson reduces the number of calls made after meeting with an energy-draining, stalling customer, top performers intensify their prospecting efforts and instead see more customers. Make the law of averages work for you.

4. We can't expect our customers to remember the high price of indecision during times of uncertainty. It is our responsibility to help them see beyond their mental roadblocks and help them restore their vision. Effective salespeople will skillfully remind their customers of their dreams and goals and help them focus on a bright future.

Uncertainty in selling can be managed. It is a normal part of our work. The tricky part is that uncertainty can contaminate our attitudes. The more we fear it, the more it paralyzes us. The more we accept it as a challenge to be overcome, the more it will help us move forward. Salespeople who refuse to get swept away by feelings of uncertainty are the ones who win sales and profit from the wholesale "head in the sand" attitudes of their fear-filled competitors. Uncertainty calls for a simple answer to a simple question: Do you choose to react like 80 percent of all salespeople? Do you choose to stay in the middle of the road and get run over? Or do you choose to respond like 20 percent of all salespeople and plow your way to new opportunities with a positive attitude and a strong sense of purpose? Remember Dr. Norman Vincent Peale's words: "If you put off everything till you're sure of it, you'll get nothing done!" Get going.

WHAT MAKES CUSTOMERS "HAPPY" TO BUY FROM YOU?

Happiness is like a sunbeam, which the least shadow intercepts, while adversity is often as the rain of spring.

—CHINESE PROVERB

Yesterday our insurance salesman stopped by to ask a few questions about additional insurance coverage on one of our policies. I took the opportunity to show him two broken headlights that I had replaced a week earlier because some rocks blew small holes in the glass and rainwater collected inside. He asked for a copy of the invoice and promised to take care of the problem. The next day the salesman stopped by and presented me with a check covering the damage 100 percent. I was delighted by the fast, personal service and talked to at least five people about this happy experience.

Economic trends have changed corporate attitudes about serving customers. The old objective to create a "satisfied customer" is no longer enough. The successful and globally competitive company encourages and expects their sales team to create "happy customers."

What makes customers "happy"? Below are 10 suggestions gleaned from sales managers at progressive companies who are leading this new trend:

1. Replace the old saying, "Nothing happens until somebody sells something," with "Nobody deserves to get paid unless and until we've created happy customers."

> The old objective to create a "satisfied customer" is no longer enough.

2. Replace the old response, "I'll see what we can do about this problem," with "What would you like us to do that will make you happy?"
3. Replace the old question, "How can I close this sale?" with "How can I make myself more valuable to this prospect?"
4. Cut your response time to any customer request in half, and you'll quadruple your chances for more business.
5. Double the time you spend listening, and you'll quadruple your opportunities for creating a happy customer.
6. Double the extra mile you walk for your customers, and you'll quadruple your referral business.
7. Stop hoping for a tangible, external reward each time you give your customer extra service. Happy customers are the result of caring and selfless service.
8. Change the old focus from "What's in it for me?" to the new philosophy of "I am on your team!"
9. Change your view of the world from "It's a jungle out there!" to "The world is filled with fresh opportunities for making my customers happy!"
10. Don't forget, a happy customer is nothing but an extension of your own personal philosophy of how you want to be treated.

THE PERILS OF SUCCESS

Success is relative: It is what we can make of the mess we have made of things.

—T.S. ELIOT

One day I received a phone call from a sales professional who made the following comment about his business: "I was glad that our company had to fight the recession. It was a rude wake-up call, and we had to scramble and take a hard look at how we were conducting business. Success did not teach us anything, but failure taught us to ask better questions. Today our sales staff is down by 30 percent, but our sales are up!"

It seems that life sends us two teachers: One lectures when we're successful; the other, when we fail. The teacher we get when we're a success reinforces how much we know and fills our minds with pride. At the height of his prosperity, King Nebuchadnezzar said, "This is the great Babylon which I have built by the might of my power and for the glory of my majesty." Like many other prosperous and successful people, the king spoke in language filled with "I's" and "my's." When the mind is flooded by thoughts of oneself, the wisdom of others is drowned in conceit. Great success paves the way to illusions of omnipotence and feelings of self-sufficiency. That's the time when people who were once thought of as shrewd, clever, and brilliant begin to make terrible decisions. A look at *Forbes'* list of the former super-rich who have lost their fortunes provides ample evidence. That's the time when companies that were once thought of as innovative, powerful, and dynamic begin to lose their luster. That's

·how People's Express vanished, Ford Motor Company lost millions through poor acquisitions, and General Motors lost market share. The triumphs of success seem to drive out vigilance, thrift, and industry. As a result, informed decision making atrophies, costs go through the roof, and productivity declines. When successful man-

The triumphs of success seem to drive out vigilance, thrift, and industry.

agers think that they are in the business of enjoying the fruits of success, they begin spending the company's resources like drunken sailors.

Recession has a sobering effect on many companies. The new teacher has quietly entered the back door, asking these new questions about the basics: How can we deliver more value? How can we reduce costs? Why don't we deliver what we promised? Can't we find a better way to do this job?

New work attitudes have emerged. Teamwork is in, quality is in, productivity is in; office parties are out, waste is out, and procrastination is out.

The new teacher speaks softly. When people slow down, he quietly reminds them of the number of unemployed Americans. When costs edge up, he simply flashes last year's bankruptcy statistics. When someone gets too excited about a big sale, he simply says, "No big deal, remember Mr. Deal Maker, Donald Trump!"

As we recover from the hangover of a boom economy, more attention is paid to serving customers, and managers listen more carefully to the messages salespeople collect from the field.

We've entered an era when new rulebooks are being distributed. Some of these rulebooks are printed in Japanese, German, Spanish, or some other foreign language. Global competition is one of the best teachers the American economy has had in the last decade. Success in the global village demands a grassroots effort. It starts with increasing our focus on the customer. One reader offered this simple reminder as the best advice for improving business: "Remember, the customer is our employer!"

THE SELLING POWER OF SERVICE

To serve is beautiful, but only if it is done with joy and a whole heart and a free mind.

—PEARL S. BUCK

When I looked out the window of Japan Airlines' 747 departing for Tokyo, I noticed the ground crew forming a beeline, waving good-bye to the departing plane. I asked the flight attendant about this unusual custom, and he pointed to two flight attendants waving back to the ground crew. He explained, "We're all part of the same team, and we care about each other just as much as we care about our customers."

During the 14-hour flight, I witnessed many situations that confirmed the attendant's words. The crew approached each passenger in a friendly, polite, and considerate way and served each meal with a refreshing smile. What was even more remarkable was that the crew members were eager to help each other serve the customer. For example, when I asked a question about the bus schedule from Narita airport to my hotel in Tokyo, the attendant wasn't sure. Another attendant noticed her puzzled look and stepped into the scene, hurried to get two large directories, gave one to her colleague to check, and searched through the other one. Within seconds, they produced the answer to my question. They were both relieved that they had accomplished their mission of creating another happy customer.

Japan Airlines was just the beginning of many pleasant surprises that a customer can expect when traveling to Japan.

Item: Most hotels in Tokyo employ hostesses to usher people into elevators. Long before you approach the elevator, they press the call button for you, they bow as you approach, and their gloved hands direct you to the open elevator, holding the door until their passengers have entered. All large department stores offer elevator hostess service.

Item: After I say good-bye to Prudential's president, Kiyo Sakaguchi, I am escorted downstairs by his secretary. As we arrive in the lobby, she asks me to wait for a moment. I ask why, and she says, "It is cold outside. Please wait here while I go outside to get a cab for you."

Item: During a ride on the bullet train, the train is quiet; there are two stereo speakers built into the headrest and six audio channels to choose from. A smiling hostess hands out menus and enters the order on an electronic notepad which communicates instantly with the restaurant car. Within eight minutes, the meal arrives on a tray with a receipt that has the seat number printed on it.

Item: Yodobashi Camera store in Tokyo. The ground floor is laid out in a way that makes shopping a fun experience. You can try out every single camera in the store. Imagine over 1,000 feet of counter space, camera after camera lined up ready for your hands-on inspection. The staff stands behind the counter, smiling, bowing politely as customers walk by. You are encouraged (not pressured) to examine any camera you wish. The salespeople stand by to answer your questions, and their technical expertise is just as astonishing as their command of English. I buy a zoom lens and receive my credit card receipt with a smile and a small gift box. The salesman says, "This is a small gift for you as a way of saying thank you for shopping with us."

I witnessed many more examples that testify to the willingness of Japanese people to serve with a smile and to create a pleasant experience for their customers. The best example of the selling power of service I witnessed was when I spent an entire day with a top Japanese insurance agent. Sunumu Nakamura is a

> If you find a job you love, you'll never have to work a day in your life.

sales superstar, and watching him with a customer is like witnessing a top athlete break a world record. Like all top salespeople, Nakamura loves what he does, and he loves happy customers. Nakamura explained to me the secret to good customer service when he quoted the old saying, "If you find a job you love, you'll never have to work a day in your life." After a moment of reflection, he added, "Good service begins with inner excellence."

HOW DEDICATED ARE YOU TO BECOMING A SUCCESS?

Walter Cronkite once said, "I can't imagine a person becoming a success who doesn't give this game of life everything he's got."

Superachievers like Cronkite know that you can't win 100 percent with less than 100 percent dedication.

Although many people dream about becoming a success, few do what it takes to turn their dreams into reality. They see their jobs as nothing more than work, and wonder why they don't succeed. To be dedicated means to give oneself completely to a goal, without expecting immediate gains.

Those who have dedicated themselves to their work don't do their jobs because they get paid, but because they love what they do. Ron Barbaro, former president of The Prudential, said in a recent interview with *Selling Power*, "I love what I do, and what I don't love, I like a lot."

Is the secret to success just in doing what you love and loving what you do? No, it also requires faith that your long-term payoff will be success and fulfillment. You may argue that it isn't practical to invest everything you've got into your work just on faith. Think about your life now. Are your half-hearted ways of reaching for success getting you anywhere?

If the answer is no, why not improve your chances for success through dedication and faith? Consider Elbert Hubbard's advice: "Do your work with your whole heart and you will succeed—there is so little competition."

Have you ever noticed that people who are not dedicated to anything don't advance, never change, and stay always the same, while people dedicated to their work get transformed by success?

> **People dedicated to their work get transformed by success.**

Success tends to change and transform people. In the early stages they still may be preoccupied with getting more for themselves, but as they become more successful, they often discover that giving of themselves can be more thrilling than the getting. The idea of helping others succeed has been the key message of successful people for ages. The industrialist Andrew Carnegie once said: "No man becomes rich unless he enriches others."

Inventor Thomas Edison once told a reporter: "My philosophy of life is work, bringing out the secrets of nature, and applying them for the happiness of man. I know of no better service to render during the short time we are in this world."

Abraham Maslow suggested that each person has a hierarchy of needs that must be satisfied, ranging from basic needs like food and shelter to love and self-esteem and finally to self-actualization. As each need is satisfied, the next higher level in the hierarchy becomes the target of our ambitions. Maslow argued that healthy and successful people are able to satisfy the highest-level needs, and they become self-actualizers.

Maslow's theory promises fulfillment but also brings a question into focus: "Is your glass half-full or half-empty?" You are the only one who can provide the answer. But behind that old question is a new question: "What if you were able to increase the size of the glass?" The idea was once suggested by Dr. Viktor Frankl, who said, "Human existence always points beyond itself. This I call self-transcendence—going beyond oneself." Dr. Frankl introduced the idea that we can become more than what we are now. We can transcend beyond our old selves—thus increasing the size of the glass—and our ultimate challenge is to fill the glass, and life, with meaning.

THE BENEFIT OF OBSTACLES

Concentrate on finding your goal, then concentrate on reaching it.

—COLONEL MICHAEL FRIEDSMAN

A wise philosopher once commented that an eagle's only obstacle to flying with speed and ease is the air. Yet, if the air were withdrawn and the proud bird were to fly in a vacuum, it would fall instantly to the ground, unable to fly at all. The very element that offers the resistance to flying is at the same time the condition of flight.

The main obstacle that a powerboat has to overcome is the water against the propeller, yet if it were not for this same resistance, the boat would not move at all.

The same law—that obstacles are conditions of success—holds true in human life. A life free of all obstacles and difficulties would reduce all possibilities and powers to zero. Obstacles wake us up and lead us to use our abilities. Exertion gives us new power. So, out of our difficulties new strength is born.

Ed McMahon is a typical example of the obstacle/power relationship. His fascinating story illustrates that people who succeed best in the end are frequently the ones who had the most difficulty at the start. Ed McMahon is proud to be a salesman. He discovered his ability to sell because of the financial obstacles of his modest background. His family moved so often that he went to 15 different schools before high school. The obstacle of having no friends increased his power to make

> A life free of all obstacles and difficulties would reduce all possibilities and powers to zero.

friends easily, and today he is a friend to millions of Americans.

A closer acquaintance with the life of successful people almost always reveals the presence of some unusual obstacle, bitter disappointment, or personal deprivation. As Ed McMahon's personal account suggests, there is no misfortune that a resolute will may not transform into an advantage. Out of an obstacle comes strength; out of disappointment comes growth; out of deprivation comes desire.

To achieve success means looking for the obstacles that wake up the powers within *you*.

ARE THESE HIGH-TECH MIRACLES FOR REAL?

The economic and technological triumphs of the past few years have not solved as many problems as we thought they would, and, in fact, have brought us new problems we did not foresee.

—HENRY FORD II

Today, its almost impossible for sales professionals to do their jobs without using some type of technology. In order to truly understand how this technology actually helps us do our job, I'd like you to help me with a few questions about the paradox of sales automation:

1. Why does the most advanced computer on the market always cost about $5,000?
2. Why are the most advanced products always on a waiting list because of one single part that is missing from one single supplier? (If they are so smart that they can assemble computers, why aren't they smart enough to buy parts from more than one supplier?)
3. Why do engineers always design a product that is "user friendly" yet has so many features that even their brightest salespeople can't remember how it works?

4. Why do program glitches always appear when salespeople show the latest product to their most important prospects?

5. Why, when a salesperson's computer breaks down, does it turn into an automatic excuse for not making calls that day?

6. Why do so many people mechanically stare at the screen while the computer takes precious minutes to perform a task? (Can't programmers flash a message on the screen that says: "Go do your job!"?)

7. Why do so many salespeople spend hours making an endless number of aesthetic refinements on a proposal letter while they spend no time at all checking their spelling? (Can't sales automation programs have spell checkers similar to those in word processing and desktop programs?)

8. When salespeople have a problem with their software, why do they prefer to solicit the advice of three or four of their (even less knowledgeable) co-workers before they muster the courage to call the help line?

9. Why can't computer makers install two hard disks in each machine? The prices for hard disks are lower than expensive backup units. At the end of each day, the computer could automatically write the entire database to the backup drive. If the primary hard drive crashes, the backup drive could take over automatically.

10. Why can't notebook computer makers offer two-sided screens? One side for the salesperson to see, the other side for the customer to see from across the desk?

11. Why do high-tech manufacturers tease their customers with products that offer nearly unlimited choices but frustrate their salespeople because unlimited choices create interminably long sales cycles? Why can't manu-

facturers design products that are easier to understand and easier to sell?

12. Why do salespeople who now save time through sales automation spend more time than they have saved examining new high-tech products? Are we getting so busy looking for new ways to save time that we have no time left for doing real work?

> Why do salespeople who now save time through sales automation spend more time than they have saved examining new high-tech products?

13. Why does setting up a new computer system to perform a simple job such as printing a single label take more time than typing 200 labels on a regular typewriter?

14. Why are the keys to solving a problem often more complex than the problem itself?

15. Finally, how can we take advantage of the increased productivity that technology offers without getting stuck in a high-tech muck?

THE ESSENCE OF SUCCESS

*Life's like a play: It's not the length, but
the excellence of the acting that matters.*

—SENECA

As publisher of *Selling Power*, I have conducted many interviews with Superachievers who have offered their blueprints for personal and professional achievement. Although each person's success story is unique and different, there are seven core qualities that most Superachievers credit for their success:

1. **The ability to work hard with your heart and with your head.** Think about what causes you to work. If the answer is money, you are probably working too hard for the wrong reasons. People who love what they do feel more satisfied because they don't want to waste their time doing anything else.
2. **The realization that we can't harvest the fruits of our labor every day.** Even Superachievers experience slumps. For example, Jack Nicklaus went through a two-year period where he did not win a single major tournament before winning the U.S. Senior Open. Winners are winning because they keep on keeping on.
3. **The ability to think.** Superachievers use their thinking skills three ways: (a) creatively: to shape their future; (b) positively: to enhance their motivation; and (c) confidently: to learn and recover from setbacks. The sooner you begin to think more effectively, the sooner you will act and feel differently.

4. **The ability to care about yourself and others.** Super-achievers care deeply about other people's needs without neglecting their own. They engage in regular exercise, follow a healthy diet, and manage their emotional health by connecting with positive people, reading positive books, and reaching out to help other people.

5. **The ability to grow and change.** While losers keep repeating the old themes of their lives (avoiding change, avoiding risk, avoiding new learning, and avoiding success), Superachievers keep on reaching higher and higher. They sharpen their business skills; they improve their relationship skills; and they are committed to ongoing improvement and professional excellence.

   They have realized that growing means temporary pain, but they keep on growing because they know that not growing means permanent pain.

6. **The ability to assume responsibility for your success and failure.** Superachievers view themselves as the authors of their lives. Every new day reveals two new pages in the book of your life: The left page is authored by the outside world over which you have no influence or control. The right page is empty, and it is only filled by what you choose to write. Losers leave the right page empty and complain about the left page. Winners complete the right page, and over time their entries will influence what will appear next in the book. While losers meet with failure by default, winners meet with fame and success by determination.

7. **The conviction that success is a process.** Most Super-achievers believe that success is the result of a process that is learnable, repeatable, and achievable. The essence of success is like the source code of a com-

> There are seven core qualities that most Superachievers credit for their success.

puter program that contains a long series of precise instructions. Superachievers use every important experience as a lesson for learning more about their source code of success. Some of these learning lessons come at a great price; others are handed to us as a gift from people who have learned from their own successes or failures. Every day offers us a new chance to upgrade our source code of success.

WHICH SALESPERSON WOULD YOU HIRE?

Hiring a new salesperson can be a real challenge. From my own experience with selling and recruiting and training salespeople, I've come to the conclusion that there are three basic categories of salespeople: drifters, lifestyle supporters, and success achievers. This classification is not based on scientific data, yet it may help you sharpen your focus the next time you interview a candidate. Here is how you can identify the three categories:

1. **The Drifter.** His or her résumé shows at least five different employers during the past four years. Drifters may tell you that they dabble in real estate in their spare time, or they may confess that "If I don't make it in selling, I always can go back to teaching" (or nursing, or whatever). Drifters gravitate toward selling because they like people. Some of them have good sales abilities and they like sales training, but unable to develop strong roots, drifters move in and out of companies and professions. To them, selling is just another way of making a living while they are waiting for bigger and better dreams to turn into reality. Unfortunately, drifters rarely do more than what is necessary for survival.

2. **The Lifestyle Supporter.** The biggest telltale sign? A flat salary history. When you wonder why there is so little difference between the applicant's compensation

> Drifters rarely do more than what is necessary for survival.

over the last three years, you have a vital clue that you are dealing with a lifestyle supporter because this person is better at seeking comfort than at seeking solutions. Lifestyle supporters have little desire to grow after they've reached a certain production level. Although lifestyle supporters will tell you they are competitive, view selling as their career, and love what they do, their track record indicates that they'll never rock the boat, never go the extra mile, and take few risks. Such applicants are friendly people, easy to get along with, and have only two dislikes: change and growth. With their speedometer needle permanently stuck in the "average" range, they just love cruising on a plateau.

3. **The Success Achiever.** You'll rarely find a résumé from a success achiever in your incoming mail. It travels by word of mouth. On occasion, it is sent by fax or by messenger, but only if you've specifically asked for it. Success achievers have done research on you and your company. They don't have to look for a job; they have their eyes fixed on success and growth.

Although they have had extensive training, they view themselves as self-improving learning machines. They are eager to work for a company that recognizes their talents; they like to work with (not for) a manager who will respect their independence; they have a burning desire to pursue bigger opportunities and test their mettle in new challenges and tough problems. While success achievers are self-motivated, a good mentor can help them expand.

One of our subscribers recently told me of how he advised a young success achiever: "If you want to succeed, be the first one in the office in the morning and the last one to leave. Smile a lot and ask your boss to give you more work." Within five years, she became a vice president with a six-figure income. Unfortunately, in most companies, 80 percent of the sales force is made of drifters and lifestyle supporters and only 20 percent of success achievers. These are the salespeople who make the difference between finishing first and just finishing.

THE THREE KEYS TO SALES SUCCESS

The key to success isn't much good until one discovers the right lock to insert it in.

—TEHY HSIEH

There are three key factors that are critical for competing successfully and maintaining sales success: knowledge, skills, and motivation.

1. **Knowledge.** To make buying decisions, today's customers demand more detailed information. Salespeople need to know more than raw data; they must know where to obtain the right information and deliver the information to the customer in the shortest, most comprehensive, and most compelling way. The two most critical challenges in managing sales knowledge are (a) keeping up-to-date with the latest information that is important to the customer and (b) keeping up-to-date with sales automation tools designed to speed up the communication process with the customer. In order to keep up with rapid changes in the field, we have no choice, but to aggressively exploit technology so that we can manage information faster and better.

2. **Skills.** Research has proven that good selling skills are the result of ongoing learning, coaching, and practice. While salespeople often claim to have many years of ex-

perience in selling, on closer examination, their level of skills is often nothing more than one year's worth of experience repeated over and over. Effective sales managers continually train and rehearse their salespeople's skills to avoid lost sales. All sales superstars study, practice, and polish their skills.

Take Zig Ziglar, for example. I recently visited with him right after he gave a two-hour presentation to a record-breaking audience of 16,500 in Dallas, Texas. He told me that although he had given the same presentation a week earlier in Houston, he spent four hours studying and practicing his speech before appearing in Dallas. Why? Because when he gives a performance, he gives it his 100 percent best effort. The same applies to our sales performance. If we stop practicing, we lose our winning edge, and soon our performance will drop. If we run only at 80 percent of our capabilities, we will lose 20 percent of our sales opportunities.

3. **Motivation.** Without motivation, even the most knowledgeable or skilled salesperson can't win. A well-motivated salesperson will develop positive qualities like enthusiasm, confidence, persistence, determination, and discipline. These qualities are easy to identify but tough to maintain over a long period of time. What makes motivation so challenging is that salespeople are often unaware of their own motivational difficulties. They often say that they are doing great when they actually could benefit from an encouraging talk or a pat on the back. A salesperson's motivation is like a plant in a garden. The plant has roots that can't be seen; they represent the salesperson's past which can't be changed.

Over a long period of time, the sales manager can help the salesperson create stronger roots (a stronger

> Over a long period of time, the sales manager can help the salesperson create stronger roots.

sense of identity). As the stem of a plant moves toward the sunlight, salespeople move toward challenging goals and attractive rewards. The sales manager has to help salespeople reach those goals and provide appropriate rewards. And just as most plants have the capacity to bloom, most salespeople have the capacity to reach profitable levels of success.

HAVE YOU PLANNED FOR YOUR SUCCESS?

It is a bad plan that admits of no modification.

—PUBLILIUS SYRUS

Most people like performing their jobs much better than they like the job of planning. Yet planning plays a large role in how we perform over a lifetime.

Mary Kay Ash once said that most people plan their vacations better than they plan their lives. She is right, because most people, including top corporate executives, think in short time frames. While some people concentrate only on doing the things they like doing, successful people use the power of planning to ensure growth and prosperity. Each year they plan to build and expand on their successes.

Peter Drucker once wrote about how a manager must develop long-range plans: "He must keep his nose to the grindstone while lifting his eyes to the hills. . . . he not only has to prepare for crossing distant bridges—he has to build them long before he gets there. And if he does not take care of the next hundred years, there will be no next hundred years—there may not even be a next five years."

Dun & Bradstreet reports that the median age of U.S. firms is only 12 years. According to a study of 614 family business own-

> Three-fourths of companies don't do the planning needed to shape their futures.

ers by Massachusetts Mutual Life Insurance Co., only 8 percent of all family businesses make it to the third generation or beyond. The study revealed that business longevity depends largely on planning: strategic planning, business planning, and succession planning. William O'Hara, director of the Institute for Family Enterprise at Bryant College in Rhode Island, commented in *Small Business Reports*, "Three-fourths of companies don't do the planning needed to shape their futures."

What do we dislike most about planning? The answer is simple.

Many plans go wrong. What do most people do when their plan fails? They give up on their goals! That's a mistake. When a plan goes wrong, we must only change the plan, not the goal.

The French writer Victor Hugo once offered this piece of advice: "He who every morning plans the transactions of the day and follows out the plan, carries a thread that will guide him through the labyrinth of the most busy life. The orderly arrangement of his time is like a ray of light which darts itself through all operations."

If you realize at the end of the day that your plan from last night has not materialized, sit down and draw up a new and better plan for tomorrow, but never give up on your goal.

Plans may also go wrong because they don't fit the circumstances. General George Patton wrote in his book, *War as I Knew It*: "One does not plan and then try to make circumstances fit those plans. One tries to make plans fit the circumstances."

No matter why our plans fail, we must develop bolder and better plans. Some people are afraid to make big plans. They don't dare to test their mettle, nor do they dare to tempt their fate. Among all professions, architects tend to plan ahead more than others. The British architect Daniel Burnham told the London Town Planning Conference in 1910: "Make no little plans; they have no magic to stir men's blood and probably they will not be realized. Make big plans; aim high in hope and work, remembering that a noble, logical diagram once recorded will never die, but long after we are gone will be a living thing, asserting itself with ever-growing insistency. Remember that our sons and daughters are going to do things that would stagger us."

Those who never plan ahead work too hard all their lives, and most of them never end up with anything to show for it. Go ahead and plan for a more successful year. Most people won't do it. Will you? Make bold plans that will stagger your grandchildren.

SELLING IS CHANGING—FASTER!

hen people ask me how we can manage changes in selling I usually answer this way. There are two types of changes sales executives need to master: changes within their own companies and changes in the business world. Let's discuss them one at a time.

As companies grow, they move through three major stages of growth. First is the pioneer stage, where salespeople are like missionaries trying to convert the nonbelievers. The biggest challenge is to keep motivated and to believe in your future success. Second, the power stage, where sales are growing in the double digits, where demand outstrips supply, and where people think that they are 10 feet tall and bulletproof. The biggest challenge is to remember that the paying customer—not you—is number one. Third, the plateau stage, where one product looks like the next, where creativity is at a low, and where the organization spends more time on analysis than action. The biggest challenge is to remember that salespeople can make a critical difference—but they must change (like the organization they work for).

In the pioneer phase, we must change to adapt the sales approach to the needs of the untapped market. In the power phase, we must change to become more professional. In the plateau phase, we must creatively adapt the sales organization to get better—or get beaten.

A good way to look at the changes within the business world is to look at the evolution of the automobile from the Ford Model T to today's latest model car. Here are a few fundamentals that have not changed: The steering wheel is still round, cars still have brake pads, we still use a combustion engine, and each car has a set of four wheels. Just about everything else has changed.

The fundamentals of selling have not changed since Ford salesmen talked about the benefits of an automobile over a horse-drawn carriage. It is still the salesperson's job to find customers, to identify their needs, to help solve their problems, and to get them to agree to purchase. The need for personal, human contact will always drive the fundamentals of the sales process. Everything else is subject to change.

Let's go back to the automobile industry: Today's steering wheel works more efficiently with power steering, the airbag adds to the safety, larger engines make cars go faster, power brakes make slowing down easier, and automatic traction control makes driving in snow more efficient. As a result of these changes, today's new cars are safer, faster, more powerful, more convenient, more comfortable, and more enjoyable to drive. These changes were driven by one big goal: to increase customer satisfaction, which is the best way to sell more.

As technology has improved cars, telephones, and computers, the profession of selling has changed and improved as well.

Today's salespeople are moving information faster; they give their customers more choices; they offer more value without being asked; and they change and adapt the sales process to match their individual client's needs. To keep winning, we must keep improving and changing. Business thrives on change. Without change progress is impossible.

Fifteen years ago, there were few salespeople who used the computer as a sales tool; today, over 75 percent of our readers are planning to purchase their second-generation notebook computer.

Five years ago, professional certification was not a hot topic. Today, there are many different organizations that offer

> **As companies grow, they move through three major stages of growth.**

sales certification programs. Why? Companies want it, customers demand it, and many salespeople strive to be more professional.

In your company, the bottom line depends on how well you change and how fast you are able to change. In the world of business, change is at the heart of progress. Since the rate of change is increasing everywhere, it is best to make change your friend. Former Prime Minister Harold Wilson once said: "He who rejects change is the architect of decay. The only human institution which rejects progress is in the cemetery." That's where the cigar-smoking, back-slapping, joke-telling salesmen of yore are now resting in silence.

LOOK FOR EAGLES

We do not see nature with our eyes, but with our understandings and our hearts.

—WILLIAM HAZLITT

I recently purchased a sea kayak to explore the shores of the Potomac River near my home. Each weekend I discovered new creeks, beaver dams, and an abundance of wildlife—ducks, geese, swans, osprey, herons, and deer. One weekend, when I entered a small creek, I saw a doe crossing a creek up to her ribs in water. I surprised dozens of turtles sunning themselves on the muddy banks and watched a bald eagle catch a fish. There is no greater sight than observing nature in its pure form. To me, the greatest sight of all is the bald eagle.

Another Saturday I covered about 12 miles along a protected creek and spotted 11 bald eagles. I am in awe of their capacity for greatness.

When eagles take off, they use every muscle and every feather for maximum power and speed. Their vision is legendary. They are efficiency in action. They zero in on a goal and don't let go until it is in their talons.

While there are many eagles around us in society, just like the bald eagle, they are not easy to spot.

I recently met an eagle, former POW Paul Galanti. He spent nearly seven years in a North Vietnamese prison camp. If you think that what you are facing in life right now is tough, check yourself (in your imagination) into the "Hanoi Hilton" for one night. Just imagine how much you could learn about dealing

> There is no greater sight than observing nature in its pure form.

with adversity. Galanti soared above unbearable adversity and earned eagle status for life.

I see the word *EAGLE* as an acronym: Eagles are Enthusiastic and exuberant about life; Eagles Aggressively attack adversity; Eagles are Genuine and gracious with others; Eagles Listen and learn; Eagles are Earnest and effective in everything they do.

I encourage you to study eagles, to observe their habits, to absorb their lessons, and to apply their skills in your daily life. I promise, you'll soar to new heights. Take off today, retrace the flights of these eagles, and feel their uplifting spirit under your wings.

DON'T LET THE ECONOMY SLOW YOU DOWN

To dispose a soul to action we must upset
its equilibrium.

—ERIC HOFFER

A friend who is in charge of sales of an automotive dealer-
ship recently complained about the slowdown in car sales.
As he showed me his sales records, I looked over his
shoulder to scan the activity on the showroom floor and on the
car lot.

While there was not a single customer in sight, there were
five salespeople waiting for customers to drop in. One studied
the local newspaper; another concentrated on *Sports Illustrated*;
numbers three and four observed the traffic outside; and number five just sat there, staring into space.

The sales manager explained that other dealerships confirmed that business has dropped off. He also mentioned reports from several automotive manufacturers that indicated a
nationwide downward trend in automotive sales.

I asked the obvious question, "If business is down, why
aren't your salespeople busy making calls? Instead of waiting
for customers to show up, why aren't they calling their old customers and getting new leads?"

Caught by surprise, the sales manager said, "You're right;
they should do that. But why should I be the one to tell them?

> How do your
> salespeople react to a
> slowdown in sales?

Why can't they think of this on their own?" I answered, "Because as the manager you are in charge of what to do and how to do it. If you tell your salespeople that you expect them to call 40 customers a day, and if you give them a good script, they'll be sit-ting behind their telephones making calls. If you provide the what-to and the how-to, they'll follow your direction. If you wait for them to take the initiative, nothing will happen."

How do your salespeople react to a slowdown in sales? Here are five tips to avoid a performance slowdown in a slowing economy.

1. **Persistence pays off.** Sales managers who set high standards for persistence won't enable their teams to walk the path of least resistance. It's the sales man-ager's attitude that determines the attitude of the sales team. If your attitude says "we'll persist" and "we'll re-spectfully decline the invitation to the next recession," then your team is likely to win.

2. **It does not really matter where the economy is going—what matters is where you are going.** If you are clear about your goal, if you know how many calls it takes to close a sale, if you do whatever it takes to reach your goal, you'll do well in any economic cycle.

3. **Boost the motivation to win.** Create a short-term in-centive program to reward extra effort. You'll quickly re-alize that the economy is not driven by the interest rates set by the Fed but by the interest sales managers show in motivating their teams.

4. **Get back to basics.** Nothing can spoil a sales team more than success. If last year was great, chances are

that your salespeople are already skipping vital steps in the sales cycle. They may leave out the cost-justification step, make shortcuts in their presentations, or use weak closes. If sales have slowed down, it's time to sharpen the ax and start a boot camp sales training program.

5. **Get more creative.** When business slows down, salespeople are hungry for new ideas. Good sales managers know that problems are nothing more than wake-up calls for creativity. Schedule a brief brainstorming session every week. The goal: to improve every single process within your sales organization. When business slows down, let your creativity lurch into overdrive. Just a few new creative selling ideas will pull your sales forward to the fast lane.

MESSAGES CAN FIZZLE OR SIZZLE

You have to regard a presentation to people as a bit of a performance.

—JOHN CLEESE

What is the number one problem that stands in the way between you and your prospect? Chances are that your sales messages fizzle in the marketplace. Prospects don't know you, your company, or your product; they don't understand your message; and they don't care about your story or your unique selling propositions.

Back in 1888, very few people had heard of George Eastman and his little black box that he called the "detective camera." Only a few people understood photography, and even fewer knew his company. He started a sales revolution with the simple and compelling message, "You push the button; we do the rest."

Since 1888, advances in technology have created a landslide of products and an avalanche of information. Today's customers are bombarded with sales messages they have learned to tune out faster than ever.

Ask direct marketers and they'll tell you that every year direct-mail response rates decline. Today, more than 99 percent of all direct-mail letters are ignored. Ask sales managers and they'll tell you that up to 90 percent of all prospects ignore a salesperson's attempt to close the sale. Ask yourself, how many sales presentations did your team make and how many resulted in a sale? Ask marketing managers and they'll explain that 60 percent of all marketing materials are ignored by the salesperson.

> Every market has its own jargon, acronyms, and buzzwords that salespeople need to know.

Why do most sales messages fizzle? Because we seem to be better at creating new products than we are at creating clear and compelling sales messages.

What makes effective customer messages sizzle? In 1937, the first author to write about selling with sizzle was Elmer Wheeler. His book, *Tested Sentences That Sell*, revealed his experiments with sales messages and their impact on prospects. Wheeler spoke about "meaty words" that prospects could sink their teeth into and "watery words" that had little impact. For example, Wheeler found that if a waiter asked, "Would you care to order a red or white wine with your dinner?" it would double the sales of wine. Today's customer-message management has less to do with the right choice of products than with the right choice of words. Every market has its own jargon, acronyms, and buzzwords that salespeople need to know. Each prospect lives in a different world that is governed by different preoccupations, perceptions, and preferences. While a CEO's perception focuses on the future, on strategy, and on efficiency, the CFO's preoccupations revolve around cash flow and ROI. For a sales message to gain access to the prospect's mind, it must reflect the language of the market, the preferences of the prospect, and the challenges of the company.

GETTING SQUEEZED?

*Difficulties are meant to rouse, not
discourage. The human spirit is to grow
strong by conflict.*

—WILLIAM ELLERY CHANNING

With the economy still sputtering and CEOs keeping a tight lid on spending, sales managers report that paths to decision makers are blocked with obstacles, which is frustrating for the entire sales team. Here are six proven coping strategies from a number of seasoned managers:

1. **Real opportunities are harder to identify.** Most sales managers direct their salespeople to explore opportunities with companies that are doing well. What happens many times is that salespeople are not doing so well in capturing these opportunities. Why? Because the decision-making process has migrated upward, and salespeople are struggling to make connections with these upper-level executives. The solution: Bring higher-level executives to make joint calls with your salesperson.

2. **Real solutions are harder to justify.** Many times salespeople propose a great solution that will do wonders for their client. The only problem is that the client does not see enough benefits to justify the purchase. Why? Because many companies are still in a budget-saving mode and don't even think beyond the current quarter. The solution: Spend more time mapping the pain

points in the earlier phases of the call. Ask the client to put a dollar figure next to each pain. Justify the economic wisdom of your solution by using your client's numbers.

Offer a clear vision of the future and create a solid plan.

3. **Friendly relationships are not always productive.** Some salespeople work hard on making every call a pleasant experience. Yet they are often surprised when a competitor calls on their client and walks away with a sale, leaving them empty-handed. Why? Because some salespeople have a strong need to be liked, and their need for approval prevents them from asking some of the tough questions that would advance the sale and actually help the customer make a favorable decision. The solution: Get these salespeople to switch from the "farming" style to the "hunting" style. If coaching fails, move them to customer service.

4. **With sales being slow, it's more difficult to cut off problem clients.** While sales managers preach that every sale counts, they often fail to count the time and expense it takes to close certain sales. The solution: Give your sales team clear directions when to say no to a client.

5. **When business is slow, creative ideas are harder to find.** While it's easy to say that sales problems are nothing but wake-up calls for creativity, salespeople are often hard-pressed to come up with new ideas for increasing sales. Why? Because they think that they've tried everything under the sun. The solution: Pull in your top performers and list all the best ideas that worked for them. Then ask your top performers to act as mentors to your sales team.

6. **When business shrinks, salespeople get confused about your expectations.** Why? In tough times, salespeople worry more about their jobs and their income. The solution: Don't add to their stress with unrealistic expectations or ambiguous leadership. Offer a clear vision of the future, and create a solid plan that leads to new opportunities. Salespeople respect what you fairly expect and impartially inspect.

THE DO NOT CALL REGISTRY– WHO WINS?

The recent creation of the National Do Not Call Registry had the telemarketing industry locking horns with lawmakers who decided to protect their constituents from receiving calls at their homes as they sit down for dinner. Now that more than 30 million consumers have signed up to stop unwanted calls, who are the real winners in this war over privacy?

It's clear that the telemarketing industry has lost a valuable selling opportunity. Industry experts estimate that thousands of telemarketers will be losing their jobs. Many of them are single mothers and handicapped people. Worried about getting fined, American businesses are now exporting telemarketing jobs to India, and they are saving a bundle in the process. While a telemarketer in the United States earns about $50,000 per year, a telemarketer in India is happy to perform the same job for only $5,000.

Are the consumers protected from all telemarketing calls after they sign up with www.donotcall.gov? No. Political fundraising is exempt from the rule. Calls from charitable organizations are allowed, and companies can still call consumers to conduct telephone surveys. There are few clear winners in this ongoing battle, but many losers.

The question is: How could the industry have prevented this battle and avoided the heavy losses? Is there any hope of reversing the law in the future?

Unfortunately, telemarketing firms know a lot about making

> Assume for a moment that these millions of telemarketing calls would help cure cancer.

calls based on a rigid script, but they seem to know little about creative selling. If they had thought outside the box, they could have turned the lawmakers into friends and created a situation where everybody wins.

Lawmakers see the telemarketing salesperson as a leech, a thief of time who calls at night, interrupting the family without offering an obvious benefit.

Someone who thinks outside the box would take a closer look at the lowly leech and start the creative-thinking process. Isn't the leech one of humankind's oldest recorded medical remedies? Even today, surgeons use leech therapy after reconstructive surgery to help restore blood circulation. Since a leech produces its own anesthetic, the procedure is usually painless.

What if we could apply that model to telemarketing? What if the industry attached an unquestionable and pain-relieving benefit to every telemarketing call made in the United States? Let's assume for a moment that these millions of telemarketing calls would help to cure cancer, AIDS, or other formidable diseases that threaten our society? With all its IT power, the industry could easily collect one penny for every call made to a consumer. Over the course of a year, these pennies might add up to $100 million that could go directly to help the thousands of people who are suffering. With a little national advertising, the ring of a telemarketing call would be as welcome as a giveaway prize patrol.

Within a short time, the consumer telemarketing call would no longer be seen as a leech that steals time but as something that contributes to the greater good of society. Isn't that what selling is all about?

INFORMATION-BASED SELLING

Nobody knows enough, but many too much.

—MARIE VON EBNER-ESCHENBACH

The chief complaint of many sales managers is that the old ways of selling no longer work. Yet there are a number of companies that enjoy increased sales and profits. What is their secret? These companies have deployed their internal information assets to help improve their customers' businesses. They've discovered that good business information is often the deciding factor for buying a product or service.

A vice president of sales recently said to me, "Information has changed how we sell and what we sell." Think of it: At the heart of every management decision is good information. Information determines how we connect with our customers. The quality of the connection hinges on the company's information universe and how it can be mobilized to enhance the customer's business. Take UPS, for example. In the past, a UPS salesperson sold package delivery services. Today, the UPS salesperson is the customer's trusted advisor who diagnoses business needs and offers business-enhancement solutions. These solutions may involve inventory management, supply-chain management, call-center management, warehousing, packaging, shipping, invoicing, collection, or financing the customer's business. While UPS customers still enjoy the brown truck pulling up at their loading dock, of real value to them are the business information and ser-

> Review your information assets and deploy them to help your customers.

vices UPS delivers to the manager's desktop.

Take Hilldrup, a United Van Lines agency. A few years ago, the sales team called on HR departments to sell corporate relocation services. Today, the Hilldrup salesperson analyzes the client company's relocation information management process. Most companies don't have a central information utility that can seamlessly organize the moves of hundreds of executives. That's where Hilldrup can leverage its information asset in the form of a relocation Web portal. This extranet site allows companies to track shipments, manage moving costs, update insurance policies, or post employee relocation guidelines. Hilldrup still loads furniture into trucks, but what the customer enjoys most is that every relocation question is answered by a comprehensive information utility.

Take SAP as another case in point. In the past, SAP salespeople sold enterprise software solutions to IT managers, using tailored presentations that took many days to prepare. Today, SAP salespeople are able to connect seamlessly with customers regardless of language, title, or level of IT knowledge while reducing the number of steps in the sale. How? The sales team benefits from a sales and marketing intranet site that serves up customer messages segmented by industry, by customer expertise level, and by company size. With a few mouse clicks, a salesperson can create a customized presentation CD that reflects the prospect's primary interests. SAP salespeople can easily get in sync with their prospects' information needs and get faster decisions to implement their highly adaptive solutions. After all, people love to buy from salespeople who can deliver relevant and accurate information without delay.

It may be time to review your information assets and deploy them to help your customers understand your business and improve their business. The world is no longer beating a path to the door of those who create the best product, but instead, to those who deliver the most useful information.

ARE YOU SELLING AT EVERY LEVEL?

If a man be self-controlled, truthful, wise and resolute, is there aught that can stay out of the reach of such a man?

—PANCHATANTRA

While many companies promise to build their organizations around the needs of their customers, few companies can claim that they organize themselves around the needs of their salespeople. Yet the two are inevitably linked. In a sales-focused culture where the entire company—not just the sales department—is involved in selling, salespeople are more successful, and customers are more satisfied. Such highly successful companies as Dell, UPS, Ritz-Carlton, and IBM not only create customer-focused organizations but also back up their commitment with sales-focused cultures.

What are the elements of a sales-focused culture? Ideally, a company sells at three distinct levels. At the "C" level, top executives set the tone for the organization by clearly articulating the company's mission, vision, and values. While the company's mission describes the noble purpose of the organization (selling meaning), the vision statement induces people to aim their efforts toward greater future achievements (selling inspiration). The description of the company's values provides a sensible guide for creating relation-ships (selling trust). For a true sales culture to exist, C-level executives need to continuously sell meaning, inspiration, and trust to the com-pany's employees, customers, sup-pliers, and shareholders. Research

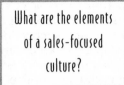

What are the elements of a sales-focused culture?

shows that companies whose employees understand the mis-sion, vision, and values enjoy a 29 percent greater return than other firms.

At the midlevel, sales and marketing departments create messages that are in sync with the company's mission, vision, and values. While marketing creates the brand promise, sales delivers by elevating customer relationship to a branded sales experience. The key to a true sales-focused culture is to have sales and marketing departments that speak with one voice.

At the street level, salespeople act as company ambassa-dors who are fluent in two languages. They speak the cus-tomer's language and their company's language. They are able to diagnose the right problems and deliver the right so-lution. Ideally, the sales team's internal and external rela-tionship skills will build a competition-proof connection between the two organizations that will ultimately extend from the mailroom to the boardroom.

To borrow an analogy from the world of music, C-level sell-ing is like an overture that offers a preview of imminent excite-ment and drama. Midlevel selling engages people with a catchy tune that resonates pleasantly in the customer's mind. Person-to-person selling is more like jazz, which is the art of the moment. Good salespeople are like jazz musicians who can instantly improvise and hit the right note at the right time to turn the right prospect into a happy customer.

Very few companies are able to act in concert from top to

bottom. It takes an enlightened CEO and a highly talented sales and marketing team to create a sales-focused culture where all members of the organization play their part in a symphony that creates delight in their customers' ears. It's easier said than done, but the results can be magic for top-line and bottom-line growth.

A LESSON ON GETTING BETTER AND BETTER

> The actions of men are the best
> interpreters of their thoughts.
>
> —JOHN LOCKE

Recently, UPS received the American Business Award for "Most Innovative Company." This was the second year in a row that UPS walked away with this prestigious award. There are very few 97-year-old, $33.5 billion companies still acting like startups, trying to improve every day. Below is a list of UPS's characteristic attitudes, created by the special mindset that drives UPS to consistent innovation and success.

1. **Employ constructive dissatisfaction.** UPS CEO Michael Eskew once said that UPS has created a corporate culture that encourages constructive dissatisfaction. This doesn't mean that UPS executives love to nag—it means they love to brag about having improved something before anyone else realized it could be done better.

2. **Act like a challenger; think like a leader.** Challengers are mission-driven, and they focus on winning over their competition. People who only "act" like leaders always face the danger of becoming too ego-centered. The consequences? They lose their edge through exces-

> Turn into trusted advisors with a mission to enhance business efficiency and profitability.

sive self-involvement. But in a crunch, top UPS executives have been known to roll up their sleeves and move packages. They are not afraid of getting their hands dirty.

3. **Expand your sales and service menu.** Every year, UPS introduces a number of new services to its customers. What's remarkable is that its expanded services are always closely connected to the core business. Successful companies know that the moment they move too far away from the core, their resources will be stretched and their focus will blur.

4. **Sell value, not price.** While there are many ways to cut corners and ship packages at a lower cost, UPS constantly creates new ways to offer more value through greater efficiency, higher reliability, greater access to information, and better on-time performance from pickup to delivery.

5. **Move deeper into your client organizations.** When UPS expanded its business to include e-commerce services, supply-chain services, and banking services, UPS salespeople learned how to move deeper (and higher) within their client organizations, turning into trusted advisors with a mission to enhance business efficiency and profitability.

6. **Synchronize your brand message.** To keep in step with the ongoing transformation of its business, UPS has synchronized its marketing message with the evolving needs of the market. The 1985 tag line, "We run the tightest ship in the shipping business," has evolved in 1993 to "The package delivery company more compa-

nies count on." In 1995, UPS advanced to "Moving at the speed of business," and in 2002 came "What can Brown do for you?"

7. **Elevate your customer experience.** Whether customers connect with UPS online or face-to-face, they will be engaged in a personal, memorable, and meaningful experience. Research by the Gallup Organization shows that companies that create high employee engagement and high customer engagement are four times more profitable than those with lower scores on employee engagement or customer engagement. That's Big Brown's hidden advantage—they deliver positive customer experiences 13.6 million times a day.

ROI SELLING

O nly two decades ago, sales managers told their sales-people, "Features justify the price, but benefits justify the purchase."

After the Reagan years, customers wanted more from salespeople than a long list of benefits before they signed on the dotted line. Soon sales managers embraced value-added selling as the ultimate activator of the decision-making neurons in the customer's brain. The new idea was to sell value, not price. The idea worked until products and services became so complex that companies had to pay outside consultants to translate a salesperson's proposal back into plain English.

During the past economic downturn, drawbridges to corporate fortresses were lowered only for salespeople who carried white papers with the magic word ROI (return on investment) in the title. ROI selling appeals to the hearts of the CFO in need of black ink and the decision maker in need of evidence that the solution will actually work.

Here are some of the steps of ROI selling:

1. **Understand your prospect's business model.** Find out how your prospect is making money now.
2. **Help your client collect data within the company to build a business case for the purchase.** For example, a fleet-leasing sales executive may help a CFO calculate the cost per mile of a fleet of company cars. To build the business case, help the customer articu-

late the "value mission" necessary to sell the idea to management. For example: "Reduce the cost per mile while increasing safety."

3. **Develop clear financial reasons for buying.** For example, IT salespeople know that technology-based metrics will be rejected by a CFO, whereas a clear focus on financial metrics moves the IT project forward.

> Help the customer articulate the "value mission" necessary to sell the idea to management.

4. **Use your financial acumen to show your clients how to calculate the ROI.** Many buyers do not have the time or the knowledge to perform accurate and objective ROI calculations. Savvy salespeople calculate the cost of not purchasing and compare it to the projected gains resulting from the purchase.

5. **Link the features of your product or service to specific outcomes and provide objective, cost-justified benefits of your solution.** The ROI-focused sales proposal often contains a value map that documents the dollar value of every part of the solution.

6. **Determine the future value of your prospect's business.** Help the customer to visualize the changes in the current business model and how it can evolve and grow into a much larger and more successful entity with your solution.

7. **Match the sophistication of your ROI analysis to the interest level of your audience.** Use the one-page executive summary when you speak to the CEO; show the

detailed ROI analysis to the CFO; share the application benefits with the end-user.

The new ROI approach requires more work up front but often leads to shorter sales cycles. Best of all, it leads to higher margins. What's not to like about that?

WHY SELLING SLOWS AS A COMPANY GROWS

There is no failure except in no longer trying. There is no defeat except from within, no really insurmountable barrier save our own inherent weakness of purpose.

—KIN HUBBARD

Every business goes through evolutionary cycles. Each new cycle brings on a new style of selling. In the entrepreneurial stages of a business, salespeople feel the passion that comes from the rush of customer acceptance in the marketplace.

The sales team is highly motivated because they are fully aware of the near-limitless potential for the new product or service. The customer is king, and the sales process follows the art of creative improvisation. There is no cap on sales commissions. The company adapts to market changes with lightning speed. Decisions are made on the fly. Gut instincts replace the need for market studies. When passion rules, the organization is as fluid and responsive as a basketball team. Offices are small, the furniture is used, and everyone works late.

As the company grows, the need for bureaucracy begins to emerge. Passion no longer comes from enthusiastic cus-

> When passion rules, the organization is as fluid and responsive as a basketball team.

tomers but from exciting incentive programs. Sales managers rationalize that consistent success demands formalized training. Salespeople must follow a standardized sales process, and a CRM system is installed. New competitors emerge, and cost cutting is necessary to finance the growing business. The company invests in market research. As more department heads are hired, decision making slows down, and bureaucracy begins to get in the way of pursuing new growth initiatives. The sales office is stylish, but uniform, and all managers work long hours.

As growth continues, the company goes public. Stock options create employee excitement—but within a year the stock loses its luster. The bureaucracy solidifies, and top executives are stressed from dividing their attention between satisfying customers and courting Wall Street. The sales organization is restructed, sales goals are set higher, commissions are capped, and rigid budget and communication guidelines are imposed. Decision making slows down, and the legal department gains more influence. The sales team is eager to set new records, but competitive price wars slow sales growth. Executives talk about the need for balance in their lives, and more employees leave promptly at 5 p.m.

As the company reaches maturity, passion is replaced with rationality. After several rounds of competitive mergers, the company is no longer leading the market. Winning is measured by staying profitable year after year. A quiet fear of losing major clients has crept into the consciousness of the sales team. The energy of the organization is sapped from playing a defensive game imposed by new mergers and new, vertical competitors. More, rigid rules slow the pace, and strategic moves are often prescribed by outside consultants. Hiring new salespeople has become increasingly difficult.

The pain of growing can often divert the attention of an organization from the customer to internal trials, troubles, and trivia. Yet there are a few consistently successful companies that continue to grow, adapt, and transform in sync with the market. Their leaders know that passion beats rationality every time. How do they keep the passion alive year after year? By keeping their goals squarely focused on what matters most—satisfying the customer.

HIDDEN TREASURES

While many companies explore selling opportunities in China, few sales and marketing executives look at the opportunity that's right at their doorstep—the Chinese-American market.

Understanding the cultural history of Chinese Americans begins by looking back at the Gold Rush of 1849, when more than 300 Chinese immigrants landed in San Francisco. Some of them found huge gold nuggets (weighing more than 40 pounds) that would provide them with a lifetime income. The good news spread fast, and over the next four years, more than 20,000 people left China to pursue the American dream. Mark Twain described the traits of these hardworking immigrants, saying, "A disorderly Chinaman is rare and a lazy one does not exist."

Today, research shows that Chinese Americans, compared with the general population, are twice as likely to start their own businesses. It is estimated that businesses owned by Chinese Americans create more than $200 billion in annual revenues. One of the first Chinese businesses in America was a Chinese restaurant that opened in 1849 on Jackson Street in San Francisco. Today, there are three times more Chinese restaurants in the United States than there are McDonald's franchises.

The Chinese-American market shows the fastest population growth rate, the highest levels of educational achievement, and a higher household income than any other ethnic group. More than 2.5 million Chinese Americans wield a spending power of more than $300 billion.

Chinese Americans spend more time on the Internet and buy more online than the average American. They are price-sensitive and brand-conscious buyers. According to Simmons Research, electronics are high on their list of purchases.

> Businesses owned by Chinese Americans create more than $200 billion in annual revenues.

As for communications, more than 500 Asian-language media vehicles target this growing market, according to New York–based Kang & Lee Advertising. Chinasite.com lists two Chinese-language radio stations in LA, one in New York, and one in San Francisco. There are a host of Chinese radio and TV programs available by satellite or from local cable companies. Since more than 80 percent of Chinese Americans speak Chinese in their homes, savvy marketers use that fact to their advantage. For example, the *New York Times* created a direct-mail piece (with the copy in both Chinese and English) and staffed a call center with a toll-free order number with telemarketers who spoke Mandarin and Cantonese. Sensitive to the subtleties of Chinese culture, the *Times* even decided to change the color of its Chinatown vending machines from the traditional blue to the culturally more effective red.

In marketing literature, it is important to avoid the number 4, which sounds the same as the word for death (*sie*). The number 8 suggests prosperity, and 888 is viewed as a symbol for growth and prosperity.

Culturally sensitive marketing is only half the key to success. Companies must also customize their sales presentations to meet the unique needs of the Chinese-American market. For example, New York Life relies on a Cultural Marketing Division to train and educate the agent team responsible for serving the Chinese-American market. The training includes sessions in estate planning and underwriting that are taught in Mandarin and Cantonese. New York Life realizes that the best way to reach the hearts and minds of customers is to speak to them in their own language—in all its forms.

COULD YOUR SALES FORCE RUN MORE EFFICIENTLY?

The really efficient laborer will be found not to crowd his day with work, but will saunter to his task surrounded by a wide halo of ease and leisure.

—HENRY DAVID THOREAU

"Efficiency is doing things right," says Peter Drucker; "effectiveness is doing the right things." To better understand the subject of efficiency, *Selling Power* did a survey of 445 top sales executives. We wanted to learn more about the most important and difficult challenges sales managers face across 31 different industries. Among the 41 questions we asked, four groups of questions deserve particular attention:

1. **Hiring and recruiting.** In this area, 57.7 percent said that, at this time, they don't have the right people in key positions in their sales organization. As the economy continues to grow, the challenge to find key people that can lead the company to greater success keeps increasing.

2. **Growing sales without sacrificing existing accounts.** In this area, 45 percent of respondents find it challenging to balance new-account acquisition with servicing existing accounts. Some try to find the solution by divid-

> Effective sales process is critical for winning more sales, yet few experts agree on how it can be done efficiently.

ing the sales team into "hunters" and "farmers" (37 percent); others provide incentives for creating new accounts (72 percent). While everybody wants to achieve profitable growth, many sales organizations find that ambitious growth targets can often inflate the cost of sales and cause a loss of existing customers.

3. The sales process. In this area, 64 percent of the organizations surveyed follow a standardized sales process, yet only 53 percent of the companies use CRM to capture vital customer information. When it comes to replicating the best practices of their top sales producers, only 46 percent are satisfied with the outcome. The majority of sales leaders agree that an effective sales process is critical for winning more sales, yet few experts agree on how it can be done efficiently.

4. **Customer insight.** While 58 percent say their marketing collateral is designed the way their salespeople sell, only 56 percent say their marketing collateral is designed the way their customers buy. In only 43 percent of the companies surveyed do marketing people go on joint calls with salespeople. While marketing insight easily cascades down from the company to the front-line salesperson, customer insight doesn't easily flow back from the field and often has precious little influence on future sales and marketing strategies.

MEANINGFUL MANAGEMENT MOMENTS

*You cannot be a leader, and ask other
people to follow you, unless you know how
to follow, too.*

—SAM RAYBURN

How can you make every moment you spend with a salesperson count? Here are some helpful hints.

In an effort to reduce the cost of sales, more and more sales managers have been forced to increase their span of control to 12 or more salespeople. With more people under their command, managers must make every encounter with a salesperson more productive, more motivating, and more meaningful. How can you make every moment you spend with a salesperson count? Here are some helpful hints:

1. **Tune in to the person.** Focus on what you can see, hear, and feel. Observe the body language. Are the salesperson's eyes downcast? Are her arms crossed? Is his voice thin, harsh, or pleasant? Is the rate of speech fast or slow? Is the pitch higher than normal? How do you feel as you survey the salesperson?
2. **Create a cocoon of concentration.** That will enable you to see and hear everything vividly and clearly. Pay attention to the emotional content of the communication. Do you sense anger, frustration, or annoyance?

> What makes the encounter meaningful is that you've facilitated learning and restored confidence.

3. **Assume a professional, confident, and friendly attitude.** If your salesperson notices that you are preoccupied, distracted, or in a world of your own, the encounter is likely to be unproductive for both of you.

4. **Empower the salesperson to speak freely and frankly.** Simply say, "Tell me all about it." Then shut up and listen while you assume a caring and active listening attitude. Your reassuring nod will help the salesperson to articulate his or her problem without hesitation.

5. **Help separate fact from fiction.** Sometimes salespeople begin their lament about a situation with an erroneous conclusion. To sort out the facts, ask for precise details, and help them to review the situation objectively.

6. **Offer reassurance.** If the salesperson is upset after a difficult encounter with a client, avoid launching into an avalanche of logical explanations, and refrain from making superior remarks like, "You should have . . . (done this or that)." Pay attention to your salesperson's feelings. Your reassuring tone of voice and your words of empathy are far more powerful than an elaborate analysis of the situation.

7. **Become the anchor in the storm.** Once the salesperson has calmed down, you can address the logical issues involved in the situation. If the salesperson is very agitated, keep your cool.

8. **Ask the salesperson to collaborate on the solution.** It is to your advantage not to hand the solution to your

salesperson on a silver platter. Ask instead, "Why do you think the customer reacted this way?" Or, "If you had to do this over again, what would you do differently?" Instead of giving away the solution, use questions that engage the salesperson in a collaborative discovery process. You may say, "Let's think about this together and see what ideas we can come up with." After you've reached a conclusion, the salesperson will feel rewarded by the synergistic effort.

9. **Share the solutions and share the credit.** After the salesperson's problem has been resolved, thank the salesperson for trusting you and for working with you on this challenge. What makes the encounter meaningful is that you've reduced the salesperson's emotional pain, facilitated learning, and restored the confidence necessary to stay productive.

10. **Be firm if you have to.** Being friendly and understanding is not helpful if the salesperson has problems with boundaries. It's your job to remind your salespeople of the rules and to let them know that you will enforce them. Sometimes the most meaningful management moments come after you've drawn the line in the sand.

WHAT CAN YOU IMPROVE NEXT?

We are restless because of incessant change, but we would be frightened if change were stopped.

—LYMAN LLOYD BRYSON

One of the most important qualities of a sales manager is the ability to think. And not only to think and reason, but also to consciously decide what to think about and what to ignore. Here are the key subjects to consider:

1. **Strategy.** As the economy shows signs of growth, savvy managers think about the strategic choices between innovation and improvement. While innovation demands investment in new ideas that involve risks, improvement demands long-term efforts to upgrade every process with the goal of achieving small but steady gains. Innovation doesn't always lead to improvement. Even successful innovations don't always translate into a sustainable business model. The dot.com economy taught us that hyperinnovation is like a shooting star that may be doomed to fizzle, whereas ongoing improvement is a shining star that lasts.

2. **People.** Good sales managers think deeply about the people that are most important to them: their customers and salespeople. Weak managers tend to think more about how to eliminate weaknesses in people; strong managers think about building on the individual

strengths of each team member. As people grow in the areas they are really good at, their weaknesses will shrink in proportion. Effective managers are strength finders and strength builders, and they grow the business based on the strength of their core products and services.

> Good managers believe that every experience in life holds the potential to add to their knowledge, insight, and wisdom.

3. **Learning.** Poor managers habitually file new experiences into preestablished mental folders without examining their potential for wisdom. Their thinking styles inhibit learning. Effective managers tend to appraise reality objectively and review every significant experience for potential wisdom. The difference lies in attitudes and beliefs. Good managers believe that every experience in life holds the potential to add to their knowledge, insight, and wisdom.

4. **Change.** Good managers think deeply about change, and they don't dwell on what can't be changed. They recognize the need for change early, communicate the need persuasively, and sell the benefits for completing the change on a fast-track schedule. What's more, good leaders always offer a process for change; they acknowledge the pain involved in the process and effectively dramatize the consequences for not changing. Good leaders know that the secret to winning lies in constant change and adaptation.

5. **Yourself.** Successful managers are not afraid to challenge themselves to grow. They question their thoughts, actions, and behaviors with an eye toward improvement.

They ask themselves such questions as: Do I build bridges between people and tear down walls between groups of people? Do I rank integrity above performance? Do I encourage others to orbit around issues, not people? Do I enjoy flattery from a safe distance? Do I strive for balance in my life? and Do I encourage others to do the same? Effective sales managers take charge of their ongoing growth. They know that ongoing self-management provides the foundation for new thoughts and ideas so that they can lead their teams to greater achievement.

PRODUCTIVITY GAINS

*He that will not apply new remedies must
expect new evils.*

—FRANCIS BACON

The CEO sets the overall vision for a company's success. By enhancing this vision with their own tactics for success, sales managers will execute the CEO's vision in a positive, productive, and profitable way. Here are four essential strategies the successful sales manager will follow to improve sales:

1. **Improve your sales process.** The sales process is the road map sales managers design to help salespeople move sales forward from lead generation to follow-up. Unfortunately, many sales managers may become so preoccupied with tracking results that they invest little time in measuring the activities that generate these results. There are tons of productivity gains waiting to be uncovered. To boost productivity, we need to look at existing procedures and work flow and compare the associated costs and time investment to the resulting value. The goal is to improve operations—to do things better, faster, and at a lower cost.

2. **Increase sales and marketing collaboration.** Many midsize companies run marketing and sales as if they were separated like church and state. Marketing often

> The best sales leaders set an example by modeling the productive behavior they expect from each team member.

produces sales collateral that does not take into account how salespeople sell or how customers buy. It is astonishing that many CEOs see marketing as not vitally important and make little effort to synchronize these departments to better serve each customer and to stay competitive. When sales and marketing collaborate creatively and constructively, the impact on the bottom line can be quite dramatic.

3. **Insist on quality customer information.** Getting users to adopt CRM solutions is still the biggest obstacle to sales force productivity. While selling requires personality traits that center around people, CRM systems depend on a different skills set—the ability to translate conversations into data and key the data into a computer or PDA. In many companies, salespeople still write information on legal pads or the back of an envelope instead of typing it into their CRM systems. Many sales managers don't hold their salespeople accountable for missing call reports. Some companies don't reimburse T&E expenses for a trip if the sales reports are not entered into the database. The best sales leaders set an example by modeling the productive behavior they expect from each team member.

4. **Raise your personality IQ.** Sales managers believe that the foundation of successful customer relationships comes from salespeople's personalities. The big question is, How can we enhance people's talents

to increase productivity? Always look for ways to measure your personality assets and to help salespeople connect with their core talents. Learn how to raise your own personality IQ, and discover how you can magnify your salespeople's potential for greater success.

ACTION PLAN
FOR SUCCESS

There can be no acting or doing of any kind, till it be recognized that there is a thing to be done; the thing once recognized, doing in a thousand shapes becomes possible.

—THOMAS CARLYLE

My Goals For:

the next week:_____

_____

the next month: _____

_____

the next quarter:_____

_____

this year: _____

_____

My Motivation Checklist:

Books to read: _____

_____

Audio tapes to listen to: _____

_____

Seminars to attend: _____

_____

Attitudes to develop: _____

_____

My Self-development Plan:

Exercise: _____

_____

Mental fitness: _____

_____

Competitive edge: _____

_____

Professional growth: _____

_____

Financial investment: _____

_____

My Time Management Plan:

To get more done: _____

_____

To organize my professional time: _____

_____

To spend more time with family/friends: _____

_____

To serve my community: _____

_____

To reduce stress: _____

_____

INDEX

© Hisham Bharoocha

About the Author

A dual citizen of both Austria and the United States, Gerhard Gschwandtner is the founder and publisher of *Selling Power*, the leading magazine for sales professionals worldwide, with a circulation of 165,000 subscribers in 67 countries.

He began his career in his native Austria in the sales training and marketing departments of a large construction equipment company. In 1972, he moved to the United States to become the company's North American Sales Training Director, later moving into the position of Marketing Manager.

In 1977, he became an independent sales training consultant, and in 1979 created an audiovisual sales training course called "The Languages of Selling." Marketed to sales managers at Fortune 500 companies, the course taught nonverbal communication in sales together with professional selling skills.

In 1981, Gerhard launched *Personal Selling Power*, a tabloid format newsletter directed to sales managers. Over the years the tabloid grew in subscriptions, size, and frequency. The name changed to *Selling Power*, and in magazine format it became the leader in the professional sales field. Every year *Selling Power* publishes the "Selling Power 500," a listing of the 500 largest sales forces in America. The company publishes books, sales training posters, and audio and video products for the professional sales market.

Gerhard has become America's leading expert on selling and sales management. He conducts webinars for such companies as SAP, and *Selling Power* has recently launched a new conference division that sponsors and conducts by-invitation-only leadership conferences directed toward companies with high sales volume and large sales forces.

For more information on *Selling Power* and its products and services, please visit www.sellingpower.com.

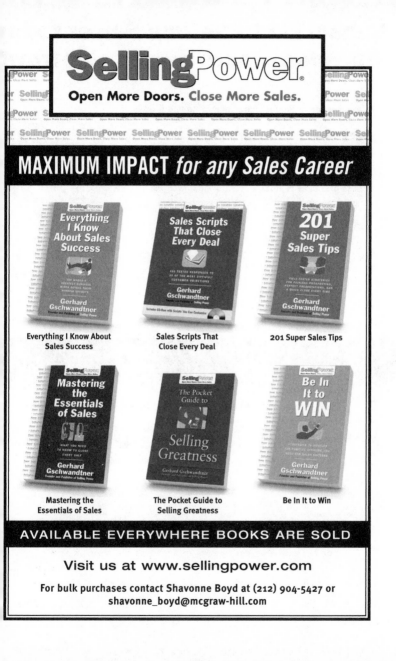

Subscribe to *Selling Power* today and close more sales tomorrow!

GET 10 ISSUES – INCLUDING *THE SALES MANAGER'S SOURCE BOOK.*

In every issue of *Selling Power* magazine you'll find:

■ **A Sales Manager's Training Guide** with a one-hour sales training workshop complete with exercises and step-by-step instructions. Get a new guide in every issue!

■ **Best-practices reports** that show you how to win in today's tough market. Valuable tips and techniques for opening more doors and closing more sales.

■ **How-to stories** that help you speed up your sales cycle with innovative technology solutions, so you'll stay on the leading edge and avoid the "bleeding edge."

■ **Tested motivation ideas** so you and your team can remain focused, stay enthusiastic and prevail in the face of adversity.

NEW!
Digital Edition
same as print.
100% online.

Plus, you can sign up for five online SellingPower.com newsletters absolutely FREE.

FOR FASTEST SERVICE CALL 800-752-7355
TO SUBSCRIBE ONLINE GO TO WWW.SELLINGPOWER.COM

I want a one-year subscription to *Selling Power* magazine.

☐ **YES!** Send me one year of the print edition for only $27

☐ **YES!** Sign me up for one year of the digital edition for only $19

☐ **YES!** Sign me up for one year of both for only $33

Please note: Subscriptions begin upon receipt of payment. For priority service include check or credit card information. Canadian and overseas subscriptions, please visit www.sellingpower.com for rates.

Name: _____ Title: _____

Company: _____

Address: _____

City: _____ State: _____ Zip: _____ Phone: _____

☐ Check enclosed   Charge my   ☐ Visa   ☐ MC   ☐ AMEX   ☐ Discover

Card number: _____ Exp.: _____

Name on card: _____ Signature: _____

For fastest service call 800-752-7355 • To subscribe online go to www.sellingpower.com